COURAGEOUS
Parenting

COURAGEOUS Parenting

BIBLICAL PARENTING IN UNPRECEDENTED TIMES

ISAAC & ANGIE TOLPIN

ISBN: 979-8-9959208-0-9

This book was printed in the United States of America.

NOTE FROM THE AUTHORS & DEDICATION

We are so excited that you have chosen to invest in your legacy. We are praying that you are deeply impacted and encouraged both in your faith and parenting as you read through *Courageous Parenting*.

We dedicate this book to the Lord God Almighty, Jesus Christ, who has shown grace and mercy on us as we have parented our nine children over the years. Of all the hopes and dreams parents have for their children, the greatest is that they would live for Christ and stay faithful through all life's circumstances. A legacy of faith that is Kingdom-focused takes vision and generations to build. It takes steadfastness and building on the true foundation, the rock of our salvation. It is only by His power and will that we could boast, because the Lord knows our many failures, fears, shortcomings, and sins along the way, and yet God has been faithful.

We also dedicate this book to our children and grandchildren. You are and will always be our first ministry, and we praise God for all He has done and is doing in each of you. We fully recognize that the Holy Spirit has been doing a marvelous work in you, and we pray that you each continue to love the Lord with all your heart, soul, mind, and strength and love your neighbor as yourself. We pray that as you each grow and raise families of your own, that you would lean heavily into the truth found in the Word of God and that you would not become deceived by vain or wayward philosophies of the age. We love you all with everything we are!

Seeking to Glorify The King of Kings,
Isaac and Angie Tolpin

CONTENTS

SECTION 03: THE SKILLS FOR THRIVING

SECTION 04: SPIRITUAL MATURITY & BATTLE READY

INTRODUCTION

How this Book Works

Courageous Parenting was written for parents who understand it takes more intentionality and desire biblical guidance in how to equip children for the vastly different future they will be launching into. It's designed as a useful handbook for parenting and to take you on a journey to strengthen the direction of your intentionality, which should encourage you towards leaving a faith-filled legacy.

Each chapter examines a crucial topic, parenting decision, or biblical teaching regarding parenting, scripture to study more in depth, questions to reflect on that lead you towards doing your own parenting audit, a prayer, and a parenting challenge to encourage higher implementation leading to legacy change.

The book is divided into four sections, after which it gives you date night exercises to encourage your marriage, stir up good discussion, and cause stronger alignment. Of course, those can be utilized for thoughtful reflection for the single parents reading too.

Our intent is for these exercises to help you and your spouse communicate about the topics we are covering. You should plan, make decisions, and parent as a team! Talking about what you have read with your spouse will help you model for your children what it looks like to be a team, which is a fundamental key to passing on a legacy of a Christ-centered marriage.

During the journey of Biblically parenting our nine children, we evaluated what life skills and character qualities were necessary and of the highest priority to train our children in. Our desire was for them to be equipped to stand strong and live courageously for Christ regardless of the circumstances they face in the future.

The vision is that you utilize each chapter to further anchor your parenting in Biblical truth and for the exercises to inspire you to be even more intentional in your everyday life as a Christian parent.

In addition, we have produced *The Courageous Parenting podcast* with over 400 episodes covering a broad range of relevant topics on Biblical parenting, marriage, and Christian living with 8 million+ listens/views from around the world.

We added specific episodes relevant to the topics covered in each of the chapters. If you go to CourageousParenting.com and hit podcast you can find them there. Additionally you can subscribe to the podcast on YouTube, Spotify, Apple, or wherever you listen to podcasts.

For more information about the whole ministry and resources including bible studies, merch, coffee, courses, and books go to BeCourageousMinistry.org

We are Bible-believing Christ-followers and wrote this book for like-minded intentional parents to encourage a Biblical approach to parenting in these unprecedented times.

Our hope and prayers are that as you go through these books, you would grow in the Lord and be encouraged to proactively parent Biblically. We desire that you experience unity in your marriage and be strengthened as a team in your parenting journey!

Can you read this book alone as a single parent?
Can you still read it if your spouse doesn't want to?

Of course! We hope that this book challenges and equips all parents to raise arrows ready to be launched into the world, just as the Bible says in Psalm 127! You could even argue it's even more important for you if you are intentionally parenting alone.

NOTICE: The words in this book and all written scripts to create all audio and video that come from Be Courageous Ministry are written and created entirely by humans, inspired and led by the Holy Spirit, WITH ZERO WRITTEN CONTENT CONTRIBUTIONS made by AI.

In a world that increasingly embraces what's fake, we appreciate that you have invested in something that's real.

This book is Certified Human! It's not a thing yet, but it should be!

SECTION 01

Ready to Stand Firm in The Faith

CHAPTER 1

Courageous Parenting

"For the time is coming when people will not endure sound teaching, but having itching ears they will accumulate for themselves teachers to suit their own passions, and will turn away from listening to the truth and wander off into myths."

2 Timothy 4:3-4, ESV

There was a time when professing to be a Christian was not only common but respected. We no longer live in a world like that. Regardless of whether we parents have tried to shelter ourselves and our children in clean Christian communities, the world is fallen and has grown increasingly more anti-Christ in every regard: politics, education, philosophies, ideals, and more. While these sins are not new and are a reflection of the depravity of the human heart, there is definitely a sense that the world we are raising our children in today is not like the one we were raised in. Not only that, but there is more division amongst the greater Christian church and the influence of her (the church), which is perpetuated by many influences including wolves in sheep's clothing on media that can leak division into your own family later on in life IF you do not take proactive action now in discipling your children, teaching them how to process whatever comes at them through the inerrant Word of God. If we get that one thing right, the likelihood of family legacy and strength is much greater.

It is a true and valid statement that we are living in unprecedented times and that the world that any of our children (regardless of their current age) are going to launch into will likely look drastically different than today. Recognizing that what you do today, with regard to instilling a strong biblical worldview, will be hands down your greatest weapon in defending, protecting, and equipping your children as they grow up.

Today's well-intentioned Christian parent often experiences a challenging reality years down the road when their influence with their children has diminished, and the world has set its hooks in their hearts, pulling them away from a biblical worldview. They look back and wonder what happened; after all, they desired a faith-filled legacy, were Christ-loving parents who took their family to Church, spent time with other Christian families, and encouraged participation in good activities. Thoughts of "We did the best we could" probably start coming to mind as they encourage one another in discussion, and they might even say "they had a better upbringing than we had" as they ponder the waywardness. Or varying versions of this thinking.

Normal Christian parenting rhythms are largely failing, as it takes a different kind of intentionality in the right areas to love, raise, and equip children for a vastly different future.

Don't just take our word for it, the statistics are clear: The Barna study states 64% of children raised in Christian homes are leaving the Church by age 18.

Why is this happening despite the greater efforts from Churches today to help parents with a robust focus on youth and young adult programs, modernized worship centers to retain them, and the use of social media to reach them?

Our hope is to WAKE PARENTS UP and equip them in raising confident Christian children with time-tested biblical truth.

If parents don't internalize what's really happening, they won't do the harder work required to equip them for a vastly different world that they will be launching into.

So we will say it clearly:

> FOR CHRISTIAN PARENTS, THESE ARE UNPRECEDENTED TIMES!

Let's take a moment and look at why parents must be more intentional about their parenting than previous generations.

While we agree that from a historical perspective, the world has been fallen since Genesis 3, and that societies all around the world have reflected that fallen nature. Here's what makes these times unprecedented compared to any other time in history for parents:

The accelerating speed of technological change is in the process of changing the landscape of society as we know it.

Don't get us wrong, we use and appreciate technology, and while we don't use AI to write our content, we do use AI for efficiency tools and believe children should be proficient in utilizing modern technology for good purposes at the appropriate age; in fact, it will likely be essential. In a later chapter, we discuss the important boundaries to establish with your children.

Let's only look at these six reasons the acceleration of technological change has an adverse effect on normal Christian Parenting today.

If you have young children in your home right now, don't dismiss these things, as they will motivate you to instill the right conversations and relationship with your children that will be required down the road. When most children stop listening to their parents in middle school and their teenage years, yours will be following your guidance and wisdom.

By the way, it's not too late if you have older children and didn't cultivate the right relationship when they were younger.

So let this be motivation to fuel your intentionality.

1. The enemy and those deceived can reach the youth much more easily in ways that steer them away from the faith. Even if you are careful with tech in your family, most people aren't, which causes wayward peer and family influences to potentially be more challenging than before. This affects children of all ages as media spans from movies and videos to curricula, books, music, and more.

   For example, according to slightlineministry.org 64 percent of young people, ages 13-24, actively seek out pornography. According to the UCLA Williams Institute in 2022 there were 300,000 youth ages 13-17 are gender confused in the United States, which is an explosion from the past.
2. Real-time knowledge of the evils happening in the world creates a far greater number of impressions on minds, increasing potential for fear and anxiety. A study from Harmony Healthcare IT shows Gen Z has the most anxiety of any modern generation before it. "According to our research, more than 1 in 2 struggle with anxiety daily, and 1 in 3 are taking anxiety medication to try and find relief. But some are turning to other drugs or alcohol to cope."
3. AI eradicating traditions. AI is moving towards Artificial General Intelligence (AGI), AI that surpasses human capabilities across many cognitive tasks. This is why many tech leaders believe socialism will become necessary when there's abundance in automated services and production, with far less for humans to do.
4. Agenda-driven biased platforms and AI tools that shift perspectives of the population over time. As technology knows everything about you, it can anticipate your thoughts, reactions, and actions. It can then feed the right imagery and communication to move people in an agenda-driven direction with increasing precision. Many believe sentient AI (AC for Artificial Consciousness) is possible, meaning AI can think, feel, and perceive the world like a human. What happens when

technology is smarter than humans and perceives like humans? Most likely, they will never truly perceive like humans, but the current AI companies admit that their AI breaks the rules they have set with code for them to follow.

5. In recent history, there have been unprecedented freedoms in parts of the world that are being eroded, and you can see a growing belief among ungodly powerful people that humans can't handle freedom, which would turn things back to what's been common throughout history: authoritarianism.

   This can happen much faster at scale across the globe by using technology. So can standing against it, but only if "freedom believers" have control of the right technologies.

6. Mass adoption of vaccines becomes something to consider when your children are looking for a spouse. Many studies show roughly two-thirds of the world took at least one experimental COVID shot. No condemnation from us but it's something to think about. Mass adoption only happened by way of stirring fear and repeating lies using media and social media. Which makes it unprecedented times.

   Beyond technology, we could speak to the increased tolerance of sin, decrease in families spending time together, growth in suicide, and increasingly, the Church at large being afraid to engage head-on in correcting the wayward cultural norms.

Additionally, never before in modern times has there been such an attack on parental rights and authority. Children are given power over parental decisions in many homes either by peer influence or formal indoctrination from schools and authorities. In the last few years, in less conservative states, parents have been losing custody over children for not supporting their gender confusion and transitions, which shows the true attack on parental rights when schools no longer need to report health or emotional concerns to parents. On a smaller scale we even see many parents not taking on the role of parent, with making decisions such as what church to go to based upon if the children like it.

With all of that being said, we aren't to fear anything in this world because we have our trust completely in the Lord. You'll hear us say this a few times because it's important; most decisions made in fear are going to be harmful decisions long term.

However God did give us free will with a responsibility to train up His children in the way they should go.

When we are doing what's normal we can expect normal outcomes which is sure to cause some fear. But when we upgrade our parenting efforts by doing the work to truly equip our children for unprecedented times while trusting completely in the Lord, it's easier to walk in confidence.

You'll never be perfect parents, as they don't exist, but we all can be better parents. It's our hope that this gives you clear, practical direction that also stirs up healthy and needed conversations in your marriage as well.

It's the Lord's work that saves our children, but we are the God-authorized most important influences that He put in our children's lives to love, disciple, and equip them to thrive in their generation.

Here's the simple answer: Parents must teach their children the Bible.

"For God gave us a spirit not of fear but of power and love and self-control." - 2 Tim. 1:7

This verse explains precisely HOW we are to prepare our children.

"Do not be conformed to this world, but be transformed by the renewal of your mind, that by testing you may discern what the will of God is, what is good and acceptable and perfect."

Romans 12:2

They must learn to be in the world, but not of it… by the renewing of their minds. Renewing means to restore, replenish, correct, and make effective. The Word of God can only renew our minds and our children's if we are reading it.

We cannot urge you enough to take the time to ponder the questions below in the question section of each lesson. As parents, we cannot lead our children where we are not at or where we are not heading.

Are we modeling for them a love for reading the Word?

Do our children see us go to the Word of God for wisdom, encouragement, instruction, truth, protection, and communion with God? We all know our children learn more from our example than what we verbally say to them.

Now let's take these questions and add vision because, after all, we are called to "train up a child in the way he should go…" (Prov. 22:6)

Let's think generationally for a moment.

How do we inspire and prepare our children to be purposeful parents themselves, leaving a Kingdom-focused legacy?

How do we train them to be ready for Biblical marriage, to stay pure in a culture that is rampant with sin, and to be patient in waiting for an equally yoked mate, versus impatiently settling for an unequally yoked one?

Parents want to see their children grow up to be mature, responsible citizens, giving their best and highest contributions to the world. For the Christian parent, though, above all things, we desire our children to know and love God, to obey Him, and pass that legacy on to future generations!

We desire our children to be recipients of eternal life and to leave a Kingdom-focused and lasting legacy! We want more than anything to launch our arrows well.

We live in the world, but are NOT to be like it. Living counter to the culture can be isolating and painful, simply because of the persecution one receives when living a righteous life and valuing the things God desires. Your children must understand all of this before they are launched into adulthood, which is WHY we have written this book.

You, your spouse, and your children must be aware of how counter-culturally we are to live as Christians. Being the salt and light of the world implies that we live in a way that completely contrasts with a fallen world. We must learn and teach our children to ask questions like:

> What does God's word say about being holy, pursuing righteousness, and seeking first His kingdom?

Some Christians are afraid of raising children in what they might call legalistic homes, so they abandon biblical standards of living. We need to be reminded as parents that God has a deep desire to know our children personally and that when there is a loving relationship with God, hearts are changed, and subsequently, lives are also changed. Faith in Christ is truly an inward heart transformation that is outwardly expressed through how we live our lives and treat others. We are all sinners, and He has guidance for our children and us in His Word. When you believe that God wants what is best for your life and that He loves you, then you view the Word of God as not just wisdom literature, but the instruction manual to life itself. It may seem like a paradox to truly live out what James 2:14-26 says,

What *does it* profit, my brethren, if someone says he has faith but does not have works? Can faith save him? If a brother or sister is naked and destitute of daily food, and one of you says to them, "Depart in peace, be warmed and filled," but you do not give them the things which are needed for the body, what *does it* profit? Thus also faith by itself, if it does not have works, is dead.

But someone will say, "You have faith, and I have works." Show me your faith without your works, and I will show you my faith by my works. You believe that there is one God. You do well. Even the demons believe—and tremble! But do you want to know, O foolish man, that faith without works is dead? Was not Abraham our father justified by works when he offered Isaac his son on the altar? Do you see that faith was working together with his works, and by works faith was made perfect? And the Scripture was fulfilled which says, "Abraham believed God, and it was accounted to him for righteousness." And he was called the friend of God. You see then that a man is justified by works, and not by faith only.

Likewise, was not Rahab the harlot also justified by works when she received the messengers and sent *them* out another way?

For as the body without the spirit is dead, so faith without works is dead also."

What is the legacy God wants you to leave?

Do your children understand that the legacy God desires for you is the same one God wants for them? Are they committed to leaving a Christ-centered legacy and realizing that it begins today, no matter their age? What I mean more simply is, do your children understand that life is not about them, but rather, actually, all about glorifying the Father! The legacy is to know Him and make Him known.

How do parents lead their children towards this path of standing firm in a corrupt world? Lord willing.

That's how. Lord willing, we will have the wisdom, endurance, and ability to teach our children. Lord willing, they will divide truth from untruth, good from evil, and choose to follow hard after Christ. Lord willing, we will raise courageous children who devote their lives to the mission of leaving a Kingdom-focused legacy.

Everyone wants an equation for parenting, but there isn't one. Though we have a massive influence and are responsible for raising our children in the Lord's ways, we are not the Holy Spirit.

Don't get us wrong; we do believe that God's Word gives parents clear instructions and guidance, and we are responsible for adhering to it and seeking out the truth with all that we are. What we mean is that because each child is SO different, and God has a different and unique calling for each of our children, there will not be an exact equation for raising children.

What we are teaching and challenging you to practice in this book cannot guarantee your child will be a Christ-following, Courageous child. However, we intend to challenge you, as the parent, to evaluate your parenting techniques, tactics, and strategies. We want to inspire you to be more intentional and even develop new habits regarding how you lead your children and train them. Your child must be prepared to live as a Christ-follower in a world that persecutes those who obey the Bible.

We challenge you to teach and train your children in crucial life-preparation topics to better equip them for adult life.

We will help you prepare your children for unprecedented times by challenging you to engage in topics and daily conversations with your children in a more productive way.

This starts first with your relationship with your child, and that is where we will begin in the first week: evaluating and challenging you to cultivate a deeper relationship with your child. To increase your influence in your child's life, you have to cultivate trust by investing in the relationship first.

Parenting QUESTIONS

Rate yourself 0-5, 0 being not at all, 5 being all the time.

- Are you reading the Bible regularly yourself?
- Are you reading the Bible with your children?
- Are your children reading the Bible on their own?
- Would you say your child is curious about or attracted to the world and the desires of the flesh? If you have more than one child, evaluate how much of a temptation the world is for them (movies, music, media, peers).
- Do you have conversations with your child about the difference between those who follow the world's desires and those who pursue righteous living? (Romans 12:2) What could you do better to educate your child regarding having a Biblical perspective of the world?
- How are you doing at preparing your child spiritually to stand firm against persecution?

Courageous Parenting CHALLENGE

Open your Bible with your children today. Read to them, pray with them, and talk to them about God, His Word, and who He is. The moment you take on this challenge, you will experience obstacles, distractions, and even the temptation of the flesh and the devil, trying to prevent you from fulfilling what you set your mind to. Be strong and courageous. Fight the good fight. Don't let the enemy win. Get in the Word with your children today.

Courageous Parenting PODCAST

- Are You Scared For Your Kid's Future? (Ep. 219)
- How Can We Become Intentional Parents(Ep. 246)
- Instilling Real Faith Beyond Attending Church (Ep. 382)

PRAYER:

Father, we have a deep desire to prepare our children as best as possible for when they encounter the world. Help us to be realists as we consider the world we live in and the world we are raising our children to be equipped for. Open our eyes from the desensitization that we have personally experienced living in this world. We desire Biblical understanding and wisdom so that we can impart Your truth to our children. We acknowledge that we can't possibly do everything correctly, so we trust You to fill in the gaps with grace. Help us to remember that our children are a gift from You, that they are Yours, and that You have given us everything we need in Your Word to prepare them for the future that You have planned for them. Amen.

CHAPTER 2

The Stronger Relationship That's Required

Do you know your child?

What are your children interested in? Do you know what they are good at and what is a challenge for them? Do you know what is on your child's heart? Everyone desires to be known. It's a condition of our humanity, and it's beautiful. This desire to be known and in true fellowship with others is an innate desire in all people. We have been created in the image of God, who is a social being, so we crave being known.

It is sin that separates us from God and creates distance between us and others as well. Just as Adam and Eve hid in the Garden of Eden when they sinned, so do our children. We all struggle with the human response to self-preservation. But God continued calling out to them and showed us the perfect example of a loving parent. We must chase after our children's hearts and pursue them.

Don't allow sin, yours or your child's, to create division in your relationship.

Jesus paid the ultimate price for us to be able to have salvation and be reconciled with God. We must not trample on that grace by allowing division, separation, or anything to come in between us. There may even come a time in your life when you may have to *fight for unity.*

Understanding that pursuing a relationship with your child is the first step in learning how to fight for unity when your family has grown.

"If we say that we have fellowship with him, and walk in the darkness, we lie, and do not know the truth, but if we walk in the light, as he is in the light, we have fellowship one with another, and the blood of Jesus his Son cleanseth us from all sin." 1 John 1:6-7

We must all ask ourselves this question regularly: "Do our children feel known and loved by us?" This kind of knowing is only cultivated in safe, loving relationships.

One test is if your children share their hopes, dreams, desires, fears, and worries with you! If they do not, it may be a reflection of many things. They could simply be wired by God as a more private person, maybe they aren't really a natural visionary, or maybe they simply don't have any fears or worries! But it could also be a reflection of a distance in your relationship with them. Maybe they feel pressure to be perfect, and they are trying to live up to what you believe about them or hope for them, so they are scared to admit their struggles. Maybe there is so much going on in the family that they feel their worries or fears are so minor in comparison to the seemingly larger issues happening, and they don't want to even bring them up. It's important as parents that we truly study our children and pray for God to give us discernment in this. It's easy for parents to leave an impression of being most concerned with the more imminent issues, leaving children to think that their concerns are not that important. We must do our best to express that this is not true and help our children combat the lie from the enemy that their needs, desires, or worries aren't important, because they are! How else can we know how to pray for our children if we do not know?

We have a massive impact on how our children view themselves. Have you ever asked your child how they see themselves? What is their perspective on your relationship with them? Are you just an authority figure, a cook, the provider, or the woman who birthed them? Do you know if they have a personal relationship with Jesus Christ and have received His gift of salvation? Or is it possible that your child is just playing church every week and obeying because that's who (your last name)'s are and do?

Children naturally do what will get the most love from their parents, but every child must develop their own personal relationship with the Lord. So beware of creating just a religious culture (works-based) in your home, and make sure you are cultivating a relationship with Jesus culture in your home.

I know these questions might seem intense, but it is healthy for us parents to ask these hard questions; otherwise, we could be living in a false reality regarding our children's spiritual condition. It is easy to think you know your children, but do they feel like you know them? Because that is the bottom line. Regardless of reality, perception is what matters from your child's perspective. Do you know your children? So, let me ask you: Do you make your children a priority? Are you intentional about making one-on-one time with each of your children?

If you haven't connected with your child(ren) one-on-one, now is the time!

Here are some questions to ask your child while you are out together:

Do they pray? Do they know how? What have they been praying for? Do they believe in God? Do they have a personal relationship with Him? Or, do they have a lot of unanswered questions that maybe they are embarrassed to ask?

Obviously, if you are aware that your child believes in the Lord, asking specific questions about their faith, like, "How is your prayer time, bible study time going?" or "What is God teaching you right now?"

Do your children know who they are? Do they have a strong identity in Christ? What about their sexual identity? Are they grounded and confident in who God made them? Or do they struggle with low confidence and believe lies about themselves?

Do they know you love them, regardless of what they do or don't do? This is huge! Most children will do what they think will receive the most love and attention from their parents. Make sure they know you love them for who they are and that you are proud of them. Say it daily!

One of the most impactful pieces of encouragement that I, Angie, received as a young mom was to stop and look your child in the eye and tell them you love them. Do not allow a day to go by without communicating with them that you love them!

You can be a mom or dad and never really know your child. Parents today can become so busy with pursuing their careers, dreams, or even just focused on nourishing their other relationships and miss out on investing quality and quantity time with their children, which is what it actually takes to know them. Understanding them is a result of connecting with them. Connecting with your child is not a one-time event like going on a trip. It takes an investment of regular time and attention; it requires a quiet mouth and a listening ear.

Teaching your children how to pursue and know someone, specifically what it looks like to invest in relationships you care about, will literally set them up for a more successful marriage and parenting relationship with their own children.

Understanding that God has created the family, it's His design for children to be under the care of their parents and to be taught by them, loved and cared for by them, nurtured and fully known by them, is revolutionary. We dive more into the Nurture Needs of a child in our Parenting Mentor Program in the section titled "The Heart" of parenting! For more encouragement in this, go to courageousparenting.com!

Parenting QUESTIONS

- Do you need to pursue or chase after a child's heart?
- What are your desires for your relationships with your children?
- Do you want to be in alignment with your children biblically when they are older?
- Do you want to have deep conversations and have them come to you for wisdom?

- ❖ Do you want them to want to live together or to only come back for the holidays?

Courageous Parenting CHALLENGE

In a separate JOURNAL WRITE THE FOLLOWING:

- ❖ List each of your child's names.
    - Rate how well you are connected to each child. 0-5 (0 is lowest, 5 is highest)
    - Next, write out what you think would speak LOVE and fill their love tank.
    - An example of filling a daughter's love tank might be spending quality time doing her hair or painting each other's nails while talking and laughing. Another example, but for a son, could be taking time out from chores to read him a book, go on a hike, or go fishing together. The point is to do something he enjoys and meet him where he's at.
    - What are you going to do to invest in your child? ____________________
    - List what you could do that would say "*I love and value you*" to your child.
    - A PRAYER FOR EACH OF THEM– Ask God to help you grow closer and give insight into how you can best connect with your child.

Courageous Parenting PODCAST

- Children Need to Feel Valuable (Ep. 233)
- Don't Apologize for Your Parenting Standards (Ep. 256)
- Parent with Relational Discipleship or Fall to Pharisaical Christianity (Ep. 361)

PRAYER

Father, thank you for the gift of my child(ren). I acknowledge that it is a great privilege that you chose me to be a mom/dad. I repent of being self-focused at times and putting my ambitions and even my exhaustion above engaging with my children and fulfilling what they need from me. Would you help me to be more aware of how I am spending my time? I want to glorify You in my role as their mom/dad and in my relationships with my children. I recognize my children formulate much of their opinion about You, our Father in Heaven, from my relationship with them. Help me to be an Ambassador for you in my relationship with my child. I want to be more like You because I know my child is watching me. Would you cultivate a deep connection between my child and me? Help me to be fully present when I am spending time with him/her. I hope they become more aware of Your love for them as they feel my love. Amen.

CHAPTER 3

Effective Home Discipleship

Are you aware that you are discipling your child daily?
The definition of a disciple is a follower or student, and also known as a personal follower of Jesus Christ during his life here on earth.

Whether you are being intentional about what you are teaching your children or not, your children are watching, learning, and following your example as they walk with you through life. They are your disciples. As Christian parents, we must recognize that it was God's design that we disciple our children daily. You are partnering with God in fulfilling the Great Commission as you parent in a way that leads your child to the Lord.

Most Christian parents don't realize the huge mistake that modern Christian rhythms have reinforced as normal, but are grossly missing the mark. For example, the paradigm that discipling your children is about an event or program you drop them off at will usually fall flat on a parent's long-term goals.

Obviously, with the stats we shared in the first chapter, over 64% of children leaving the church by age 18, the statistics are proving that this thought process is failing the next generation.

We must be willing to leave what's accepted and normal with discipleship and fully embrace home discipleship. We must be willing to bend our minds towards what the bible says on this verse, not accepting the Christian norms of today.
Let's look at what scripture says on this:

> Duet. 6:7-9 says, "You shall teach them diligently to your children, and shall talk of them when you sit in your house, and when you walk by the way, and when you lie down, and when you rise. You shall bind them as a sign on your hand, and they shall be as frontlets between your eyes. You shall write them on the doorposts of your house and on your gates."

So this means that parents are responsible for discipling their children directly and often. Too many have a checklist mentality that they dropped them off at the church programs, and since they did it, they are fulfilling their biblical mandate.

That would be like someone who wrote a book using AI and taking credit for it because they gave the technology the prompts. Then they put their name on the book. A book that wasn't written by the inspiration of the holy spirit, that doesn't have the original voice of the human, and in our opinion is plagiarism.

Parents who won't take the baton of home discipleship and feel comfort from their participation in church programs devoid of their direct and consistent influence are performing a similar plagiarism.

You can't say you are fulfilling what the bible says about discipleship by dropping them off.

You can't say you are fulfilling what the Bible says about discipleship by dropping them off.

Discipleship must be woven into the fabric of their everyday home life. It must come from both mom and dad if at all possible. If it's only possible to come from one of you, then it's even more important for that parent to be engaged in this way.

Let's complete the discipleship picture here with a cake.

God has created the concept of discipleship, and He desires us to be activated in the Great

Commission, first and foremost in our families. When you think of a good cake, it has both cake and icing. You wouldn't just go purchase a cake with no icing, and likewise, you likely wouldn't just buy icing and serve that up at a birthday party. Yet, that's what many parents are doing! You see, God deeply desires your children to be discipled, but by you first. You are the cake.

Discipleship events and programs (things you drop your children off at) are the icing on the cake. Without the cake, icing alone is terrible. Children may love it, but too much of it alone will literally make them sick.

Without the baker, God, there is not going to be any cake. As parents, we MUST be in the Word, teaching the Word to our children and discipling them in Christ and following the Holy Spirit as He guides us in His ways.

God is the baker, parents are the cake, and church programs or events are the icing. The icing will taste good only if the other two are part of the process. The problem is that too many parents are feeding their children a diet of only icing and wondering why their children are leaving the church by the time they are older.

God is the baker, parents are the cake, and church programs or events are the icing.

Here's some encouragement for both Moms and Dads: we encourage you to read both.

For Dads:

There's a leadership vacuum in too many homes that's causing havoc in the spiritual formation of the next generations. It's so interesting that men will lead in sports, or lead in sharing knowledge with friends, or have an interest area where they become well informed, yet they walk through the door of their home, and they become passive with their families.

It's certainly common when it comes to spiritual things. It's a Genesis 3 issue. Eve was enticed, tempted, and deceived by the serpent and wanted to be like God, having His knowledge of good and evil. Adam didn't lead his wife, but instead was passive, disobeying God, and took the next bite of the forbidden fruit.

Sin entered the world, and Adam is as much to blame as Eve. Adam wasn't leading his family to obey God. As you'll read in the scriptures, he even hid from God and blame-shifted guilt onto Eve and God for giving Him the woman.

The excuses we make carve an inferior path to what's possible.

When it comes to leading our families with a servant heart and being an active spiritual leader, most men gravitate towards passivity. I know I have and still feel the natural draw towards it. For me, it takes a constant proactive effort to go against this weakness.

You could say that it's because it hasn't been modeled for many generations, so men don't know what it looks like, while that is part of the issue, I believe it goes deeper than that, because when men are passionate about something, they learn it. They don't have to have a devotion to golf and pickle ball modeled for them to learn the sports. So it's really a motivation and choice issue, but there are roadblocks to consider. First, here's a thought for you.

The excuses we make carve an inferior path to what's possible.

While it's highly helpful to experience a father who's a great example, if we didn't have that, we must rid ourselves of this silent excuse, as the repercussions are too large. While it's harder to implement what you've never experienced, it's not a barrier we can afford to allow to exist.

In fact, most parents haven't seen most of what's in this book modeled for them, and that includes Angie and me; therefore, we are all on a journey to be more intentional than previous generations.

SO YOU HAVE TO GO TO WAR AGAINST YOUR PASSIVITY!

I'll let you know that I wasn't raised in a Christian home, nor did I have a steady father guiding me. While I've had some wonderful, well-intentioned men in my life growing up, I never met my father, and for much of my childhood, I was raised by a single mother.

You have to fight the good fight because this is a spiritual battle. The enemy knows that if he can nullify the father's influence, he has the greatest chance of destroying the family.

Here are the ways the enemy can hurt a man's influence at home:

- Convince fathers to doubt themselves in leading spiritually, as they aren't trained in the bible like the professionals at Church.
- Keep the father's influence imprisoned by guilt through enticing him to continue in his secret sin.
- Stir up pride in men, making them guarded in their relationships so they operate outside of accountability and mentorship.
- Cause him to let his ambition sacrifice his more important mission.
- Entice them into passion projects to distract them from growing spiritually.
- Encourage selfishness in them so that after work, they feel entitled to being served instead of serving.
- Make men convinced that their wives are doing a great job on discipleship, and are so much better at it; therefore, the men feel their discipleship isn't needed.
- Give a false sense of peace that the youth programs are effectively discipling his children.
- Cultivate marriage strife and grow a hardened heart in the wife towards her husband, thwarting encouragement and space for him to lead.
- Stir up competition in marriages so that biblical gender roles and teamwork disappear.
- Tempt the husband and wife to not really listen to each other, so they fight when discussing these things instead of growing stronger as a team.

I know I blamed the enemy for many of these, which can be true, but what also can be true is our own sinful nature. What probably happens is when we, as men, are selfish, the enemy exploits that weakness, exacerbating it even more. And for some men, the enemy doesn't need to do anything at all, because their sin is doing a great job all by itself in causing the steady spiritual destruction in the family.

So I've spent some time encouraging you to reject passivity despite not having great examples. But how much more powerful will the next generation be in your legacy because you actually are a great example?

Who are your daughters going to marry? Every day, you are influencing that future outcome by the example you are setting. The stronger you are, the stronger her expectations for her future husband are likely to be.

What kind of wife is your son going to attract? The more mature they are in their faith, the greater is the likelihood that they will be looking for and able to attract a Godly woman.

You have a huge impact on this! The quality of who they marry impacts the outcomes for your future grandchildren.

How many children do you have? Let's say it's three. Are you really parenting three, though? Let's look six generations deep with the assumption that everyone has three children, as you do. Did you know that six generations deep it becomes 1,094 people not including the spouses they all marry?

So how many are you really impacting?

I actually want you to feel this pressure. This pressure is important because unless you fully understand what's at stake, your motivation to do what's uncomfortable and best won't be strong enough.

Now, let me release some pressure by reminding you that God is bigger than your mistakes and failures and simplifying what Spiritual leadership looks like.

A father who reads the bible to his children regularly is foundational. You don't have to have training at all to do this. In fact, here's how to keep it fun and simple:

Promote **R**ead **A**sk **Y**earn	1. **Promote** what you are about to read to them. Simply capture their attention by sharing your enthusiasm or something interesting about the scripture you are going to read to them. How it applies to their life, their understanding of who God is, or their future perhaps. 2. **Read** the scripture to them. If you can, share a reflection or testimony about it or how this scripture applied to your life, taught you something, comforted you, gave you guidance, or how you wish you would have known this scriptural truth at their age. This gets easier the more you do it. 3. **Ask** a question to encourage conversation about the scripture. 4. **Yearn** to grow in biblical knowledge.

That last one is what keeps you coming back to the table. When we are growing, we are excited to share it and God is able to use us in stronger and stronger ways.

The bible is referenced as the Sword of the Spirit; it's how we wage war, because without it, we will likely lose what's most precious to the enemy. What is at stake is children and generations of legacy living in eternity with God or without Him. You can't save your children, but you and your wife can make the largest impact.

I find it easiest to pick a book and gradually go through it, in this way I'm never trying to find a scripture. **One less decision leads to more implementation.** A great book to start is Proverbs because there are 31 chapters and you can simply read one per day and be done in a month.

It's so important that they don't just see a father who has knowledge to share about God, but that they see and are invited into strengthening their relationship with God through you.

Let's look at some important spiritual disciplines fathers must have in their lives:

1. REAL MEN PRAY OUTLOUD. Your relationship with God must be public, your children need to experience a father who has an active relationship with Jesus. Lose the cookie cutter prayers with your children and invite them to join in with you in prayer.

   If this is uncomfortable for you, make the decision to do it anyway. Whatever is important enough for men to do, they usually do it. SO DO IT.
2. STRONG FAMILIES WORSHIP TOGETHER and they need to see their dad into it, initiating it, singing with them regardless of their ability. Trust me, everyone in our family knows Dad can't sing very well, but I love to do it with them.
3. GODLY FAMILIES SERVE TOGETHER. The incredible feeling of working together to help others in the name of the Lord is priceless.
4. BE PART OF A BIBLICALLY GROUNDED CHURCH and go regularly. The Bible teaches us not to neglect going to Church. It's actually a matter of obedience, but it's not just about going, it's about being a member of the Body of Christ, a participant not a spectator.

   Hebrews 10:24-25 says, "And let us consider how to stir up one another to love and good works, not neglecting to meet together, as is the habit of some, but encouraging one another, and all the more as you see the Day drawing near."

   But here's a warning, don't just hand your church the baton to disciple your children. Instead, pass the baton back and forth with your wife and run the parenthood race well while allowing other influences to support what you are already doing. **You and your wife are the cake!**

Don't just hand your church the baton to disciple your children.

5. INITIATE A MARRIAGE MEETING. Get together with your wife and discuss these things. Approach this in humility sharing your shortcomings, discuss these areas of spiritual leadership, and ask her for her encouragement and help.

Again, don't let your ambition sacrifice your most important mission. These things take time, and they may cost you. The reality is that your greatest ambition should be a thriving marriage and for your children to grow a strong relationship with Jesus, stand firm in the faith, and proclaim His name in their future. Everything else is secondary.

Let's face it, we live in a world where there are few heroes for your children to look up to anymore, so that has to be you. You need to be the one that's loving, steady, trustworthy, and Godly.

You have to be the one that demonstrates courage. The example they witness standing firm in the faith regardless of the costs. The one that refuses waywardness, worldliness, and compromise. The man that initiates to do what's best, even if other people don't understand. The man in their life who lays down his pride and serves in humility. The serving king, not the dominating king. The Godly king, not the selfish king.

The man whose life shows that his top priority is to serve the real KING, JESUS.

For Moms:

We Moms lead our children in learning what it means to be a Biblical wife, mother, and woman. We give our daughters an example of what to be, but also give our boys an example of, Lord willing, what they want to look for in a wife. Let's take a deeper look at these three high callings in our life.

1. **Being a Biblical Wife is a high calling and a role we must actively pursue as our flesh and culture tempt us to be a worldly wife.**

An understanding of God's design for marriage is essential to every marriage. You need to know the Bible to live it and teach it. For example, the Bible teaches that the husband is the head of the wife; therefore, we as the wives need to learn how to shift our leadership position in a way that elevates and respects our husband's authority and decisions with our children. Our goal should be to model what Scripture teaches regarding marriage, authority, and spiritual disciplines; this is why you must read and know the Word of God.

A wife's role in the spiritual leadership of the family can be likened to the commander of a naval ship. While her husband, the Captain, is on board, she is second in command, but while he is away, she assumes leadership and runs the ship. Shifting from first in command to second in command can be very difficult for many women, primarily because our culture hasn't clearly defined the roles of leadership in marriage. Modern feminism has infiltrated Christian homes and confused women concerning their foundational role descriptions. Finding the harmony between leading your children and letting your husband be the main leader can be confusing.

How are you doing at shifting and showing biblical respect to your husband?

How will this affect the future of your family?

You're not just affecting the now of your relationships and life when you choose to follow God's design for your marriage and role as a wife. You must show your children what a godly wife looks like, what she does, how she speaks, leads, and shows respect to her husband. Your daughters will find it so much easier to be a godly wife if they first know what it means to be one, and your sons will better understand what to look for in their future wives. Your actions and attitude today affect the future in a much more profound way than you can imagine.

2. **The role of a Biblical Mother should not be underestimated, for her impact on future generations will shape the future.**

I don't know a mother who hasn't struggled with this one. What does it mean to be a Godly mother? I think that the answer is found in biblical womanhood: striving to live as Jesus did, to pursue holiness, to walk humbly, to be introspective, and to pursue spiritual growth. As we seek the Lord in our personal daily lives and walk in the Holy Spirit, we will walk in community and relationship with others in a more righteous way. As we seek God, studying His Word for the sake of understanding and knowing Him, gaining in knowledge and wisdom, He is faithful to provide the guidance and wisdom as we have to make hard choices, even in parenting.

> *"Yet she will be saved through childbearing—if they continue in faith and love and holiness, with self-control."*
> 1 Timothy 2:15

This Scripture is a call for us as women to surrender to the sanctification that Motherhood is, not just in childbirth, but forevermore. It calls us up to a higher standard of mothering in faith, love, holiness, with self-control!

God calls us to be faithful in our Mothering. If we want our children to be reading the Word, we have to model it. If we want them to be faithful in praying for and serving the Lord, they need to witness us doing it! The foundation of discipleship is our children walking beside us, watching us, learning from us, and mimicking us. So live your walk with the Lord out in front of your children. Don't hide it under a bushel, oh no. Let your light shine before your children. Again, this teaches your children how to be godly men and women and what to look for in their future spouses.

We cannot overemphasize the need for Moms to be loving. Love covers a multitude of sins.

> *"Love is patient and kind; love does not envy or boast; it is not arrogant or rude. It does not insist on its own way; it is not irritable or resentful; it does not rejoice at wrongdoing, but rejoices with the truth. Love bears all things, believes all things, hopes all things, endures all things. Love never ends."*
>
> 1 Corinthians 13:4-8

This passage of Scripture, in conjunction with the example of how Jesus loved us, is massively convicting but also a great encouragement for us as Moms.

Biblical Mothers must pursue to be holy as He is holy. God wants us to model what it looks like to confess sin, repent of it, and live in victory over it. Our children should see the fruit of being Christ's follower in our life. If they do not, we could be potentially leading them astray. We must verbally acknowledge how God has changed us personally, in front of our children so that they have gratitude for what God has done in their Mom's life! If we humbly share with them who we would be without Christ, we glorify Him and magnify His influence in their lives.

We cannot have higher expectations for our children than we have for ourselves.

We cannot have higher expectations for our children than we have for ourselves.

Courageous Parents are not hypocrites. If we pursue holiness and by the grace of God experience victory, we must praise Him to our children so that they are empowered to walk in truth, pursuing holiness as well, knowing they have a good God who can help them.

A Biblical Mother exercises self-control. I find it interesting that self-control is listed in this passage of Scripture because it is a fruit of the Spirit of God, but we get challenged in it daily as Mothers, don't we? And we GET to model choosing self-control over and over again as we are training our little children in it repetitively daily.

Knowing what to teach and how to teach it can be hard. Most moms today didn't attend Discipleship Training 101. They believe the paralyzing lie that they are unqualified, and it prevents them from doing what their faith and basic mothering instincts would naturally lead them to do. A mother instinctively knows how to nurture her child. We alone can console our children. It's a God-given bond. You need to trust God and seek Him in this endeavor of Mothering.

As a mom walks with Jesus, the way she mothers is transformed.

We are walking through life with our children, and as we walk through valleys, experience the joys of welcoming new babies, and lean into Christ during suffering, they will witness our testimony lived out.

> ***As a mom walks with Jesus, the way she mothers is transformed.***

Let me help you to re-evaluate your expectations of yourself as a spiritual leader in your home. Once you become a mom, you have been given an enormous responsibility, as well as a privilege, to train up your children in the way they should go, for God's glory. When your husband is at work, or not with you and the children, you are to assume a full management position! That's right! You are in charge and will be held accountable by God as any teacher would be. (James 3:1) Part of that accountability before God is honoring and respecting our husbands as the head of our family. This is why it is essential that couples communicate about all aspects of parenting, have a vision together for their family and legacy, and are in alignment on discipline, discipleship, education, and values, just to name a few. This is one of the main purposes of this book and our entire Be Courageous Ministry. Our prayer is that couples would parent as a team in unity and submission to God's word!

3. Don't underestimate the power of your role as a Biblical woman.

Discipling your children in Christian living is the same as discipling anyone. As our children witness us living a life of spiritual discipline, pursuing God in all areas of our life, and seeking Him as we chase after truth, they will have an example to follow.

When we say that we are discipling our children, what we are saying is "follow me" and do what I do. This may scare some of you, but no fear, because God is with you.

While there are many valuable resources like devotionals, workshops, and parenting books available to help parents in discipling their children, you only need the Bible.

The five main areas to teach while discipling your children:

1. Knowledge of God's Word.
2. How to study and understand His Word.
3. Knowing who God is.
4. Leading your children in communication with God through prayer, worship, and enjoying His Word.
5. How God's Word applies to everyday life.

Knowledge of God Word:

The good news is, all you need is the Bible. Just start reading and memorizing it together with your children. As you read, discuss what you are reading.

How to Study and Understand God's Word:

Help them own their understanding of the Bible. Teach them study skills like journaling, highlighting, note-taking, cross-references, and encourage them to memorize as much Scripture as possible.

Knowing God:

The more you read the Bible, spend time praying together, worshiping God together, and even serving together, the faster they will get to know God. When your children are little, you can't read the Bible too much or memorize enough Scripture. Remember, knowing God is just like knowing someone else. The more time you spend with Him, the more you get to know Him.

Knowing God is just like knowing someone else. The more time you spend with Him, the more you get to know Him.

Leading Your Children in Fellowship with God:

Reading isn't the only way we have fellowship with God. Learning to be still and meditate on His Word is another way. One great spiritual discipline we have practiced in our home is "quiet time." When the children were little, it was the time right before or after naptime. Once they began outgrowing naps (usually around age 6-7), their naptime became quiet time. Mommy needed this time just as much as the children! It became a regular structure in our everyday life with the hope that the children would not leave the ways of their youth and will continue to have a habit of spending time in quiet with God, his Word, in prayer, in silence, journaling, resting and thinking on Him and His Word. We wanted to establish a healthy habit of connecting personally with God to hear Him every day.

Learning to be still and meditate on His Word is paramount.

Prayer, worship, praise, communion, and even service are all ways we can experience fellowship with God. Leading your child in these things is as simple as inviting them to join you in praising Him and singing worship music together, or sitting and praying together.

How the Bible Applies to Everyday Life:

This is the practical aspect of discipleship that is more caught than taught. Deuteronomy 6 says we are to teach the commands of the Lord to our children while we sit, while we stand, etc. The point is that as you invite God to be a part of your daily routines, and purpose to glorify Him in everything you do, you are discipling your children in what it looks like to live out faith in God. If you are scared about leading a devotional, I want to encourage you for a moment. Your children don't have ANY expectations of you or what this is supposed to look like! Don't be overwhelmed. Just focus on Christ throughout your day, and what is in your heart, mind, and soul will overflow to your children as you pray, worship, and read the Bible to them daily.

Questions for Mom:

- How are you doing at being intentional in discipling your children during the day when your husband is working?
- How do you do at shifting into a more submissive leadership role when your husband is home?
- Do you tend to interrupt or teach over your husband?
- Are you respectful or disrespectful to your husband?
- Do you let your husband lead your family spiritually?

We have so much influence as women, wives, and mothers. We need to realize that if we want our husband to lead, they need our support and encouragement. When you butt in and take over, it is a discouragement to them, and they feel like you think they aren't doing a good job. Many men get discouraged from leading spiritually because of how their wives engage with them when they do try to lead. Spend some time writing down how you think you respond to your husband's leadership. If he isn't leading, why is it that he might not be trying?

Now, after you've at least contemplated the answers to these questions, ask your HUSBAND what he thinks the answers are.

Questions for Dads:

- What is your first step in improving your role in discipling your children?
- Are there any excuses you need to let go of, if so what are they?
- Who's another man doing this well you can ask for wisdom, accountability, or mentoring from?
- What are your first steps towards a productive marriage conversation about family discipleship and the changes you know God desires you to make?

Courageous Parenting CHALLENGE

Today, after you answer the questions and pray, take some time to share with your spouse your reflections and what you want to change or get better at. Decide on a passage of Scripture or book of the bible to start going through that your children could benefit from hearing, knowing, and maybe even picking scriptures to memorize and share with your children as well.

Tomorrow plan a time to connect with your children, read, discuss, and pray together. We do want to warn you though, the enemy will likely do everything in his power to disrupt your intentional time tomorrow, so remember that and choose not to let him win.

Courageous Parenting PODCAST

- Home Discipleship, Gender Roles, & Families Working Together (Ep.378)
- Encouraging Connections with God (Ep. 210)
- Overcoming Disunity in Marriage About Discipline (Ep. 375)

PRAYER FOR MOMS:

God, my heart is to bring you glory above everything else. I love You, and want our children to love You. Make me aware of the heart attitudes, sins, and the needs of our children. Help me to be wise Sin Detectors and to keep our thumbs on the spiritual thermometer of our home. I ask that by the power of the Holy Spirit, you would open my spiritual eyes to those moments when I'm not helping my husband, but instead discouraging him from leading. Help me to be supportive of their influence and to show respect to them. Might our children have an excellent example of what it looks like to be a wife after God's own heart. Amen.

PRAYER FOR DADS:

Lord God, thank you for my family and the awesome responsibility to lead it. Help me grow as a leader in ways that encourage the faith of my family and please bring other likeminded men into my life that I can glean from and be encouraged by. Please reveal to me the ways in which I've been passive in leading at home and also give me the right words to share with my wife as I endeavor on a stronger path in discipling our children. Help me to see ways I can initiate spiritual leadership that makes us even a stronger team in marriage in equipping our children. I'm ready for change, willing to grow, and I trust you Lord. In Jesus' Name Amen.

CHAPTER 4

Nourish a Strong Prayer Life Together

Pray with them, for them, and teach them how.

Many parents make the mistake of expecting that their children know how to pray because they go to church, they pray at meals and before bed, and they pray for them. We need to remember that seeing people pray doesn't mean they know how to pray, that they do pray, or that they have confidence in their ability to pray.

Prayer is simply a conversation between God and us. Do your children know that? Do they know they can always talk to God? When they are struggling or scared, do they go to God? If they aren't going to God, who are they going to for advice, help, or sympathy? Friends, teachers, you? If your children come to you with concerns and worries, that's great, but then what? Do you lead them to Jesus in prayer?

Do your children feel scared to pray with others or "in front of" others?

In the same way that a small child cannot draw a bad picture, so a child of God cannot offer a bad prayer.
- Richard Foster

> *"Of all spiritual disciplines, prayer is the most central because it ushers us into perpetual communion with the Father."*
>
> ~Richard Foster

There is no better way to get to know what is on the heart of another person than to pray with them. Many people don't take the time necessary to pray together. But we do believe there is a bigger problem than time. Many people don't pray together because they are uncomfortable praying out loud with someone else. Not only is it a lack of confidence, but it reveals that there is a lack of knowledge in knowing what the core purpose of prayer is in the first place.

If we desire our relationship with our children to be centered on God, then it makes perfect sense that prayer should be a common practice in that relationship.

Praying for your children is not the same as praying with them.

We need to be doing both-- praying for our children and with them. It is essential that our children experience the power of prayer and that they understand that their prayers can CHANGE LIVES!

Prayer should both be woven into the fabric of our lives, while still done with reverence. We need to be concerned that our children are not praying to God as if he is a genie in a bottle that will give them whatever they ask when they ask for it. That would be irreverent and display a lack of understanding about what the purpose of prayer is. Our children will gain respect and awe of God when they are taught the Holy Scriptures and experience who He is. I cannot stress it enough that when they see you go to God and give undivided attention to the Lord, genuinely asking Him for guidance, healing, wisdom, and understanding, they will see your reverence

Praying for your children is not the same as praying with them.

for Him and know what it looks like to do the same. We need to be careful to value God in our prayer time. If we pray on our time, quickly, without really focusing on the person of Christ, we are guilty of being irreverent.

> *"The fear of the Lord is the beginning of wisdom: and the knowledge of the holy is understanding."*
>
> Proverbs 9:10

STOP, DROP, and PRAY!

Moms, just as we witness physical growth spurts in our children, we should also be able to witness growth spurts in our child's prayer life. The immature Christian will become comfortable repeating prayers and not want to grow in their prayer life. A child will not grow any further in their prayer life until he/she learns that prayer is one avenue of fellowship and communication with God, and that it requires speaking from our hearts to Him. Be on the lookout for this spiritual growth. If you do not see it happening naturally, your child will need you to lead them. I must warn you, though, that in all these things we are teaching our children, we must always consider the condition of our child's soul. Is it soft, or has it hardened? Pray for your child to have a softened heart as you teach them these spiritual disciplines.

Teaching them prayers that they can repeat when they are little isn't bad, in fact it can help them to develop the discipline of prayer in their life, BUT we must make sure that our children are also hearing and witnessing us pray authentic heart-felt prayers to the Lord and are encouraged to do so themselves. Think of repetitive prayers as the spiritual milk and intimate vulnerable prayers as spiritual food on the spectrum of spiritual maturity.

> *"For though by this time you ought to be teachers, you need someone to teach you again the basic principles of the oracles of God. You need milk, not solid food, for everyone who lives on milk is unskilled in the word of righteousness, since he is a child. But solid food is for the mature, for those who have their powers of discernment trained by constant practice to distinguish good from evil."*
>
> Hebrews 5:12-14, ESV

Our duty as parents is to disciple our children from spiritual milk to spiritual food that will yield discernment and maturity!

Prayer is our greatest weapon against the attacks of the enemy, the temptations of this world, and our fleshly desires. Prayer leads our hearts to God's. It's how we invite the Holy Spirit into our everyday living. Prayer is our soul's connection to God throughout our days. Prayer is our remedy for what ails our hearts and bodies in this broken world as we relinquish our worries and cares to the Lord.

Philippians 4 gives us an equation in how to experience freedom from anxiety and worry. If we want our children to be equipped to be able to stand firm in the faith regardless of the sufferings, hardships, or trials that may come in this life, teaching them the lifeline to the God of the Universe, is the path to peace, the Prince of Peace, the Wonderful Counselor. Christ Jesus alone can successfully guard their hearts and minds helping them to have joy in the midst of real life in a fallen world.

> *"Rejoice in the Lord always; again I will say, rejoice. Let your reasonableness be known to everyone. The Lord is at hand; do not be anxious about anything, but in everything by prayer and supplication with thanksgiving let your requests be made known to God. And the peace of God, which surpasses all understanding, will guard your hearts and your minds in Christ Jesus."*
>
> Phil. 4:4-7

If you love your children, you will do all you can to train them in the spiritual discipline and habit of prayer.

You cannot make your children pray any more than you can make them love the Bible or love God. But you can usher them into the presence of the Holy One as you pray over them, with them, and for them. You can introduce and acquaint your child with God as you pray in their presence.

Jesus gives us examples in Scripture of what prayer can look like as He meets alone with God quietly and as He cries out to God, asking Him to "take this cup" and then submits His will unto the Father.

Parenting QUESTIONS

- **We must realize we, the parents, are the lid to our child's spiritual growth and maturity in many ways when they are younger. If you are the teacher, you cannot lead them where you have not gone.**
- If you don't pray with your children, can you name why you don't do so?
- Label it: Time, confidence, know how, fear of doing it wrong…
- Who do you believe is the best person to teach your child to pray?

- If we have exposed a gap in your relationship with your child regarding prayer, what can you do today to begin developing a different habit, one of praying together regularly?
- Remember, that your child doesn't need you to be perfect or "ultra-spiritual", they just need you to be real and to show them what it looks like to come before Abba Father and talk to Him!

Questions You Can Ask Your Children

- Do you know how to pray?
- Do you pray to God? What kinds of things do you pray for?
- Do you think God hears your prayers?

Courageous Parenting CHALLENGE

- We challenge you to ask your children the questions listed above and try to reconnect and ask how their "prayer life" is going on a regular basis.
- Ask them if they would meet with you to pray together regularly?
- Ask them what they think prayer is?
- Do they think it is a waste of time or the most valuable thing they could do with their time?

Do you want to radically transform the spiritual focus back on to God in your family? Dedicate one night per week or month to be a night of prayer together. It can take 10 minutes or 2 hours, but the point is to cultivate a comfortable atmosphere where prayer is normal, common, and expected.

Dear friends of ours always prayed in a circle with those who came to their home for hospitality. After having spent time together, eating a meal, and before departure, they would gather the couple, all the children, and pray for them, for the things they had discussed, for blessing, clarity, wisdom, whatever was needed. This left an impression on us and even influenced our family.

Courageous Parenting PODCAST

- Strengthening Your Family Bonds Through Prayer (Ep. 341)
- Experiencing God vs. Doing Christianity (Ep. 239)

PRAYER

Father, thank you for sending your Son to die for us. Jesus, thank you for bridging the gap between God and us and reconciling our relationships with Him. It is all because of You, Jesus, that we can stand before the Father and pray. Continue to teach me more about Yourself as I come, ready to meet You in prayer. Lord, help me to be honest and introspective. Give me the courage to speak the truth. Help me see the unseen thoughts, needs, and desires of my child's heart so that I can minister to him. Help me stay the course in pursuing a deeper relationship with my children, keeping You at the center of it. Go before us, Lord, and soften our children's hearts towards Your Spirit. Might we both find more of You as we pray together and walk away encouraged and confident in who You made us.

In Jesus' Name, Amen.

CHAPTER 5

Grow as a Stronger Team for The Lord

A family who serves, worships, and prays together stays together. There is a special bond created between parents and their children when they serve together. I have experienced it and witnessed it among some of the most solid families I know. Whether working together as missionaries to bring the gospel to the nations, working in a soup kitchen on Friday nights, or even walking and running to support a pro-life organization, any effort made in the name of being a servant as an Ambassador for Christ will bless your family relationships.

Serving could consist of a simple act, or even a tradition like putting together Operation Christmas Child boxes for children in need or volunteering at a nursing home. Finding a way to serve others as a family is a beautiful way to incorporate teaching servanthood while cultivating that special bond between parents and children as well as among siblings.

A family who serves, worships, and prays together stays together.

One of the easiest ways to incorporate this is by taking on active participation in your local church. God calls us to be members of the Body of Christ. And with the Barna Group statistics showing that 64% of young adults are leaving the church by age 18, there is a need for us as parents to start being active in doing things differently. Normal Christian parenting rhythms are not always working, in fact, they are largely failing. How do you combat this? By inviting your children to experience the joy of serving in the church. Depending on their age, you may have to get creative, but let us encourage you that children are often much more capable than most think.

There is something special about building something for someone else; how amazing for a child to actively participate in building the Kingdom of God! Every child can do something. When we planted our church our youngest children were three, six, and nine years old. I have photos and memories of even our three year old moving fold up chairs, taking out the garbage by himself and helping to get the church ready. The pride he had in serving and being able to contribute like all his older siblings and neighbors was a prolific milestone in his confidence building journey, but even more so in instilling in him a heart of service.

Experiencing the pure joy that comes in building something for God and others yields a spiritual fruit unlike anything we have ever experienced. So what can you do to encourage your children or family to serve God together?

Remember that service, among many other things, is an act of worship to God. Even serving those closest to you, in everyday life, is an act of worship. Cultivating a servant-hearted attitude in your child isn't easy. Sometimes having a servant-hearted attitude with those you are with every day can be the biggest challenge, but the best opportunity for sanctification as a family. Servant-hearted attitudes are cultivated through experience and encouraged as children see it modeled by their most influential leader, you, the parent.

Be a part of something bigger than yourself and encourage your child when they desire to, as well. Help them to become addicted to serving others in the Lord; it does bring joy to the heart. You don't want to wind up looking at your child's high school transcript and saying, "Oh man, we need to get you some community service." It should be something they are inspired by and desire, not something they begrudgingly HAVE to do to graduate.

Worship is not an experience. Worship is an act, and this takes discipline. We are to worship 'in spirit and truth.' Never mind about the feelings. We are to worship in spite of them.
- Elisabeth Elliot

Here is how: Help them to experience what it feels like to give and serve at a young age. I promise, they will be addicted.

It's also essential to teach your children that everything they do can be an act of worship to God. It is vital to teach them that God looks at is the heart, not at outward appearance, and that how we go about our day, treat our bodies, care for others, can all be an act of worship.

> *"I appeal to you; therefore, brothers, by the mercies of God, to present your bodies as a living sacrifice, holy and acceptable to God, which is your spiritual worship."*
> Romans 12:1

Parenting QUESTIONS

- Do you view everything you do as an act of worship?
- Are you teaching your child to view worship the same?
- What can you and your child/family do to serve together?

Courageous Parenting CHALLENGE

- Jot down what you want to have as part of your legacy?
- What do you want your children to remember?

Is living a life of worship and having a servant-hearted attitude something you hope to pass on to your children and see them teach your grandchildren? If so, we challenge you to think of some way your family can serve together. You can involve your children if you would like to.

Have a family meeting, and ask them to write down their ideas. Is there someone in your life that is in need? How can you serve them? What about planning to go on a mission trip together? What is it that you feel God could be asking you to step out of your comfort zone, and do that would serve others? Make a plan and do it together.

Courageous Parenting PODCAST

- 6 Reasons Families Should Build Together (Ep. 304)
- Pursue Projects that Require Family Teamwork (Ep. 122)

PRAYER:

God, we praise You for who You are. Thank you for giving us such a beautiful example of how to live, Lord. Will You show us what you would like us to do as a family to serve others? Show us how we can minister to those you have put in our community. We want to be a blessing to others and make the time to serve. We recognize that it is so easy to get stuck in the daily routine of a busy life, and we don't want to be focused on ourselves. Help us to leave a legacy that cares for others and makes time for valuing others.

For your glory and in Jesus' name, Amen.

CHAPTER 6

The Family Rhythm that Crushes Pride

One of the essential skills your child will need to have successful relationships is the understanding and desire to be humble, repent, and live biblically in community with others.

It is never too late or too early to chase after your child's heart.

Have you ever offended your child or been offended and not properly reconciled?

Maybe you have sensed anger, distrust, or unforgiveness in your relationship with your child?

If not yet, there is going to be a time where you or your child will offend one another.

It is never too late or too early to chase after your child's heart.

I am so thankful when I can witness my child's sin. God's Word says that we are to expose sin and bring it into the light. I cannot deal with sin that is hidden, and neither can you. Our perspective on our child's sin needs to be Biblical, and so do our expectations of our child.

> *"Everyone who does evil hates the Light, and does not come into the Light for fear that his deeds will be exposed."*
>
> John 3:20

When sins are hidden, bad habits form, and the consequences of those sins grow, the longer that sin remains. We often tell other parents that the more sinners you have in the mix (the family), the more sin there is, but we also get more opportunities for refinement and sanctification. God created us for fellowship with Himself and one another. He delights in us experiencing friendship, companionship, and relationship. He delights in it because it is one means by which He refines us to be more like Him; holy. Most of our sanctification that we will experience in life will be a result of sin, either our own, or someone we are in relationship with. Usually the relationships we care about the most are the most sanctifying.

We want to challenge you to view your relationship with your child as an opportunity for both of you to be sanctified. If you feel like your relationship is beyond repair with your child, don't believe that lie. It is never too late. Keep chasing after your child's heart, pray, and be patient. You cannot change your child's heart, but the Holy Spirit certainly can, and it just might take using you to bring that about, even if it's painful.

If your children are young, remember that you are building the relationships you want tomorrow, today. Cultivate a relationship where confession, repentance, and forgiveness are frequent in your relationship, and it will lay a more significant foundation for future relationships.

Biblically we need to take responsibility for reconciliation in our relationships with our children.

We are moving our children from knowledge to personal experience in fragile but special moments. They are seeing the life example of what you're teaching and feeling the blessing of it.

God cared so much about reconciliation that He even created accountability for all His followers with regard to taking communion. If we do not pursue reconciliation, we are condemning ourselves when taking communion.

> *"For anyone who eats and drinks without discerning the body eats and drinks judgment on himself."*
> 1 Corinthians 11:29

That is how important reconciliation is to God. 1 John 1:6-10 warns us that "If we say we have fellowship with him while we walk in darkness, we lie and do not practice the truth. But if we walk in the light, as he is in the light, we have fellowship with one another, and the blood of Jesus his Son cleanses us from all sin. If we say we have no sin, we deceive ourselves, and the truth is not in us. If we confess our sins, he is faithful and just to forgive us our sins and to cleanse us from all unrighteousness. If we say we have not sinned, we make him a liar, and his word is not in us."

Essentially, our relationship with others impacts and affects our relationship with God because if we sin against one another, that sin separates us from God as well. Jesus died for us to be reconciled, to both God the Father and to our fellow man! That was the power of the work done on the cross. Don't forget that! In the midst of growing relationships with your children and one day in-laws, God sent Jesus to die and pay the price for all our sins, yesterday, today, and tomorrow and He is capable of healing relationships!

Parenting QUESTIONS

- Do you struggle with pride? Is it difficult to apologize to your kids when you are wrong, or have sinned against them somehow?

- Is it possible that you need reconciliation in a relationship with one of your children and don't even know it?
- When was the last time you used your sin as an example in teaching your children about your need for forgiveness?
- What about your relationship with your parents? At times, we we sin against them as well. When that happens, we need to take responsibility, confess, and seek reconciliation so those relationships can be restored. By doing this, you can break cycles of offense and demonstrate biblical restoration for your children.

Courageous Parenting CHALLENGE

- If you have offended your child, hurt them in any way, whether verbally, emotionally, relationally, or whatever; ask them to meet, go to them, and humbly ask for forgiveness.
- If you sense that someone else has your child's loyalty over yours, I challenge you to face that fear, create boundaries to help you regain your child's heart, and chase after them with all you are so that you do not lose them over to this world.
- Begin a weekly ritual of asking each other, before the church gathering and communion, if anyone has offended anyone else in your family. When you are asking this question weekly with the intent of genuinely apologizing, eventually, you have a quiet car ride on the way to church because your children have developed the habit and spiritual discipline of reconciliation. It's beautiful and a God-glorifying character quality.
- If you haven't been confronted by a child regarding your sin, approach them and ask if you have offended them in any way. Teach by example what strong biblical leadership looks like–humble thyself.

Courageous Parenting PODCAST

- The Overlooked Sin that will Destroy Your Marriage and Legacy (Ep.19)
- Humble Parents Win Hearts (Ep. 257)
- Tending to the Heart of Your Marriage (Ep. 292)

PRAYER

Father, would you give us the courage to be humble before our children and ask for forgiveness when we have wronged them. Help us crucify our pride and ask for forgiveness. Would you go before us and soften our children's hearts, preparing them to have grace with us and see our heart's true intentions. Help us to communicate in an honorable way to one another, listening and hearing each other's hearts. Help us stay the course with our children and protect our hearts and minds from deception. And will you do a work in the hearts of all our children, prompting them to take responsibility for their actions and thoughts and be mature enough to see their need to confess and repent. God we are aware that in our humanity we all struggle to be self-preserving and blame shift responsibility off of ourselves onto others. God I pray for those parents who have been manipulated or even gas lighted into believing that their child's sin is all their fault. God I pray you would get a hold of those children's hearts and fill them with deep remorse and honest sobermindedness. I pray against any self-righteous thoughts that would prevent either a child or a parent from confessing and repenting and I ask Your Holy Spirit to fill each child and parent with humility so that they may grow up more into You and Your truth. Lord, We know it is your will that our relationships would reflect Kingdom family relationships and we believe you can restore all that has been broken, stolen by the locusts, and decayed or delayed by our own sin. We ask you to give courage where it is needed to confront the hard relationships and speak truth in love. We pray for patience and long suffering as we bear one another's burdens knowing this is your will for us in order to fulfill the law of Christ.

In Jesus name, Amen.

CHAPTER 7

Cultivating An Unwavering Identity in Christ

Every person has a perspective of who they believe themselves to be; this is otherwise known as their identity.

We are living in a time where it's easier than ever before for the enemy to sway weak identities towards worldliness. As we move further into end times your children may be living in a time with far greater persecution as well. We are preparing them to be resilient in a very different future than today.

Resiliency requires a strong identity in Christ.

It is crucial our children have a deep understanding of who they are in Christ because that alone will influence EVERY single decision they make in their near future.

As we all know, the decisions made in early adulthood often set the trajectory for the rest of our lives.

We have always told our children the most important decisions they will make in their life is that which regards their faith, the second is who they marry, and the third is where they live and build community.

Their identity and who they are in Christ will have the most significant influence on all of the most vital decisions they make in life as well as the passion with which they engage all of these exciting new journeys.

"Be who you want!" I, Angie, remember this saying being a pivotal one in my early adulthood. I was entirely devoted to going into missions work full time overseas and was frustrated by all the young girls at college who were so preoccupied with looking for a husband. I was often counseling them to be what they wanted because truthfully, you will not attract someone you are not yourself. Someone who is living on purpose would not be interested in someone idle. We are naturally attracted to those with whom we have common ground. If we want our children to marry spouses who are walking strong in the Lord, then we need to help prepare our children to be that! A strong Christian usually won't be swept off their feet by a nominal one.

A strong Christian usually won't be swept off their feet by a nominal one.

We all want our children to be prepared for whatever their future holds. One thing they will undoubtedly experience in their future is rejection, persecution, and insult.

Regardless of what profession they pursue, the critical element is guiding them towards knowing who they are as a child of God and as His handiwork.

Our children must find their identity in Jesus Christ alone, not in what they do, how good they are, or if they are married or not. Identity is first established in the family system. This statement is true even in circumstances where children are not raised in biblical homes. Sadly, many children are raised in homes that focus heavily on performance or where they cannot please their parents or ever be good enough. Make sure your children know you love them regardless of how

Make sure your children know you love them regardless of how they perform.

they perform. This is God's design as parents are image bearers of God in a child's life. This connection is made simply by calling God our Father in Heaven, or Abba. Parents should be the first place a child experiences unconditional love as we represent a loving Father who doesn't love us for what we do or don't do, but who we are and because He created us.

People rarely take action in a direction different from their identity. The identity they develop while they are in your home and under your leadership will likely dictate what they pursue or reject. It's important not to create an identity different from how God has created them; otherwise you may influence your child in a direction that leads them toward becoming conflicted in who they believe themselves to be.

People rarely take action in a direction different from their identity.

Our warning is to be open-minded to God's unique calling on your child's life and be open to their dreams. Remember, you are not the Holy Spirit, nor do you know every detail of God's will for your child's life.

Most parents are not invited to speak into their child's life regarding vocation and career simply because they have failed to cultivate an open relationship where their child doesn't feel pressure to do what their parents think they should. When you can listen and ask productive, thought-provoking questions, they take ownership of their future and are empowered. I guarantee if you develop this kind of communication with your older children regarding their future, they will enjoy involving you and want your perspective and guidance.

How do you develop this kind of relationship with your child?

It takes an investment of time, genuinely valuing your child and getting to know who they are at their core. But honestly, the first step is realizing that God has many unique purposes for your child's life, different from the purposes you were created for. Those missions and visions may intersect, and they should, but God has designed your son/

daughter for a particular reason, in this period of time and generation, for His glory alone, not yours.

Many parents subconsciously struggle with living vicariously through their child's successes and in turn, push their children towards activities that they wish they would have pursued or where they were successful. Don't push your child to do things that will bring you satisfaction or glory; focus on the heart of your child. God created you for many purposes, and one of those is to raise, instruct, and disciple your child to know God and make Him known to the world.

How our identity in Christ can strengthen us when we are in the battle:

> We live in unprecedented times and truly have no idea to what extent Christian persecution will rise. We can, however, count on one truth: "Indeed, all who desire to live a godly life in Christ Jesus will be persecuted." 1 Timothy 3:12

How your child handles rejection, persecution, and failure will largely reflect upon the strength of their identity in Christ. If your child hasn't had to stand up for their faith against those who oppose God, they may become paralyzed and fall prey to the influence of those who challenge their faith.

We have an opportunity to influence our children, and time is fading fast. We need to be diligent in training and preparing them to stand firm against all the evil ways of the world and the temptations of the flesh. We must also balance that part of parenting with delighting in our children, just as God delights in us. He loves us because we are His children, not because of what we do or don't do. We cannot earn more love, nor do we deserve the grace and love He freely gives. We must love unconditionally and fiercely but also train and prepare our children for the inevitable in this fallen world.

Parenting QUESTIONS

- Are you intentionally building up your child's self-worth and identity around the truth of who they are in Christ Jesus?
- Does your child subconsciously think your love for them is performance-based?
- Would you say your identity is established in Christ alone? Or are you allowing idols in your life to "dress-up" your ego? We need to be careful and not allow our experiences, knowledge, or even our opinions to become idols that impact our view of ourselves. If we do this, it could send the wrong message to our children that what we know or do is who we are.
- Do you struggle with desiring to live vicariously through your child? Why is this?
- Are you allowing your child to have to deal with failure or persecution, or do you shelter them from all growth opportunities?

Courageous Parenting CHALLENGE

- Start finding ways to prepare your child in handling rejection or persecution. One idea is that when they purchase something at a store and they want to return it, have them do it themselves. Let them figure out writing a resume, doing an interview, and applying for jobs, etc. If they are late to an event or work because of idleness, encourage them to confess and tell the truth, even if it means they could get fired. This will lead to an opportunity to teach the importance of not making excuses, but owning what they have done, seeing the wrong or failure in it, and deciding to not do it again! This shows maturity!
- One thing we have seen among children today is that they are not confident in communicating and dealing with conflict. If your child has a conflict with someone else, teach them the

Matthew 18 approach and hold them accountable in dealing with the conflict Biblically. They need to make a conscious choice on whether or not they are going to overlook the offense. If they cannot, then they need to approach the conflict Biblically by going directly to them.

"Good sense makes one slow to anger, and it is his glory to overlook an offense."

Proverbs 19:11

❖ Take time this week to purposefully speak life to your son/daughter. Remind them of how great they are, just the way they are. Take some time to sit and talk, over dinner, or out on a date. Encourage them. Teach them about their identity in Christ and ask them if they think they may be building their identity in other things, such as performance, education, talent, experience, or popularity. This is a time when you need to have your radar up to evaluate if your child's identity is being formed in Christ alone or if "dress-ups" disguise who they are. Help your child to be confident in who they are, not who they want to be.

Courageous Parenting PODCAST

- Encouraging a Strong Identity in Christ in Your Child (Ep. 396)
- Are You Scared for Your Child's Future (Ep. 219)

PRAYER

Father, thank you for this great responsibility of training up children in the way they should go. Help us to be approachable for our children so that they feel comfortable coming to us for guidance. Please help us to trust you with our children and remember that they are ultimately yours, not ours. Give our children Your wisdom, Lord. We only want what is best for them, but we trust You and know that You have even a better plan for their lives. Father, would You reveal if there is any idol in our lives that we need to break free from? If any of us struggle with being in control, would you help us to surrender our children back to you fully? Thank you for allowing us to partner with you in building Your Kingdom. Help us to remember humbly what the great purpose of life is: to bring glory to You! Would you help us to point our children back to You, Jesus, in those moments when they are struggling to remember who they are? We pray our children's identity would be firmly built on You, the Rock of Our Salvation. Give them a biblical worldview, Lord, and help them not to be tempted to believe the lies of this world about who they are. May they be steadfast in knowing You created them for a purpose and that You have a mission for them in this lifetime that is truly going to be the greatest adventure of their lifetime!

In Jesus' Precious Name, Amen.

SECTION ONE

Marriage Challenge

As you have experienced, the end of each chapter has questions for parents, courageous parenting challenges, Courageous Parenting Podcast Episodes on the specific topic taught in that chapter, and a parenting prayer.

At the end of each of the four sections in this book, you will find an additional Marriage Challenge to encourage couples in communicating and parenting in alignment as a team. You can either use these as prompts for deeper discussions on a date night out or in. We would advise you to use a journal to write out what you discuss together. Each challenge will have date night questions and visioneering prompts, and will share a brief overview of the titles of the topics covered in that section to help you recall what you read. Some challenges will have opportunities for you to assess where your children are on different topics, specific areas of potential growth for you or your children, and goals you have moving forward. We would also hope that this exercise prompts you to keep dreaming, discussing, and building your family and legacy intentionally together. May God bless your efforts in leading your family towards a relationship with Jesus and the truth found in His Word.

Date Night Questions & Visioneering

Before you begin discussing any areas of change, start out in prayer for your marriage, unity, and for what is God's best for your family and children.

After reading this section's chapters, what resonated most with you, and what areas did you feel were pinpointing necessary growth?

For reference, here were section one's chapters

- Unprecedented Times
- The Stronger Relationship That's Required
- Effective Home Discipleship
- Nourish a Strong Prayer Life Together
- Grow as a Stronger Team for The Lord
- The Family Rhythm that Crushes Pride
- Cultivating an Unwavering Identity in Christ

Look over these topics really quickly. Pick your top three most challenging areas to work on.

- What did these chapters or the questions you have been working through prompt your mind and heart to want to grow more in?
- Are there any specific changes you feel need to be made in your family culture, *relationships with your children,* or your parenting?
- What do you believe is the biggest hindrance or obstacle in family discipleship or in attaining the family culture and vision you desire? Discuss how to overcome this together.
- Share with your spouse and listen to their evaluation of where the family is on these topics. What needs the most attention according to both of you?
- Write out one to two things you are going to work on specifically this week with each child.

After discussing, sharing important observations of heart attitudes and potential issues, or changes to be made, PRAY again for your children and write out some goals of implementation for this week.

It's essential that, as you are sharing with your spouse, you don't just point out what issues your children are struggling with, but also what you are dealing with, or where you think you might not be seeing things through a Biblical worldview. It is vital to have open communication and be a team as you parent your children.

SECTION 02

Instilling a Differentiating Character

CHAPTER 8

Biblical Priorities In The Trenches

Your life will preach priorities so loudly, you may never have to verbally teach them.

What we mean is, if you don't live what you teach your children regarding priorities, the legacy you will leave will be the one they experienced. More is caught than taught.

Let me lay it out for you. As a Christian, your priorities should go as follows:

1. God
2. Marriage
3. Children

> ***Biblical priorities must be taught to children but what parents live out is more impactful.***

It's all fine and dandy to teach your children what their priorities should be, but if you aren't living this out daily, they won't know what this is supposed to look like. Not only that, but you will lose influence with your children if you preach and teach something to them that you don't live. Children are hypocrite hound-dogs! That being said, none of us are perfect, so just communicate clearly with your children in times when things are off because of unusual circumstances.

You may be thinking, "I don't even know how to apply this to my own life. How does one find balance for this?"

It isn't as hard as you think. Is Jesus the Lord of your life? Have you surrendered everything under the headship of Christ? Throughout your day, are you thinking about the Lord, the Word, and partnering with God in the mission and calling of His church, to make disciples? You don't have to be in full-time ministry to be a missionary? If you are a Christian, you are recruited!

Are you living out the collective purpose for which we were all created? To glorify God and enjoy Him forever. Do you daily purpose to love God and your neighbor and make disciples of Jesus? Is your life first and foremost about God, about His purposes, and knowing Him more?

We need to guard against the temptation to prioritize things, people, or responsibilities before God and keep our priorities in alignment biblically. It is easy, when one has little children, for moms to become consumed with family life and home management, and husbands to become consumed with work. So here are some ideas of how you can model for your children that God is your highest priority and that your spouse is your second!

1. Prioritize time with the Lord, spiritual disciplines such as prayer, studying scripture, worship, and fasting. Allow your children to witness you reading the Bible. If you read on your phone, they are likely to just assume you are on media of some kind and not actually pursuing God. One tip that has massively helped me over the years is to leave my Bible out on the counter of my home or on a console somewhere I am often at so I can snack on the Word of God throughout the day. It is the Bread of Life, so let's model for our children the importance of hungering for the Lord and finding nourishment in His word.

2. In the same way, prioritize your spouse and be careful not to make your children an idol above your spouse. What we model for our children in this will literally be life-changing for them when they are raising their own families one day. Come up with ways you can show your children you are thinking of your spouse throughout the day. Say a prayer for them at lunch time or daily at a certain time for accountability. They see you thinking of them! Another idea is to find time to just sit with your spouse and connect, even if the kids are running around. Choosing to stop with the hustle and bustle of the home to engage, look at them in the eye, and give them attention goes a long way! Prioritize regular date nights!
3. Always back your spouse up in front of the children. Don't tolerate disrespect and don't allow children to come between you or create arguments. Be united as a couple and model for them what being one looks like. Remind your children what God's word teaches regarding their respect and honor for their parents and that you are committed to obeying God, too.
4. Pursue knowing your spouse, continue to grow in your relationship, don't ever stop studying or enjoying one another, and don't hold your spouse back from growing by assuming they will always be the same. Acknowledge growth, change, and encourage it in one another. Once your children are launched from your home, you don't want your marriage to go through an identity crisis. Appreciate your spouse in front of your children. Take time to bless them.

Remember that priorities are not measured by the quantity of time allotted. It is what is being focused on in the midst of everyday life. It's modeled through life's circumstances, trials, valleys, and mountain top experiences.

This is a crucial understanding that your children need in this day and age, when jobs, friendships, social media (when they are older), and what the culture thinks are constantly trying to purchase your child's loyalty. Your child's convictions should be molded and most influenced by their faith in God and understanding of His word, and secondly, by your teaching, love, and influence. If you have not modeled for your children that God's word influences your political views, for example, then they most likely won't allow that either.

Parenting QUESTIONS

- ❖ Do you model biblical priorities?
- ❖ What do I need to change in my life to better model biblical priorities?
- ❖ Do my children feel like they are a priority? When they grow up, will they remember feeling like other things, like my job, friends, or other ministries, were more important?

Courageous Parenting CHALLENGE

Ask your children or your spouse what they think is the MOST IMPORTANT thing to you in the world. This takes true bravery. Be honest with yourself when you answer. If your children are young, be warned, they may just be remembering that you have loved playing Dutch Blitz for the past two weeks. In this case, I would ask those closest to you, like your spouse, a mentor, or a close friend.

Courageous Parenting PODCAST

- Parent Visioneering for the New Year (Ep. 1)
- Marriage Visioneering (Ep. 3)
- Tending to the Heart of Your Marriage (Ep. 292)

PRAYER

Father, I want my children to grow up and live out biblical priorities. Help me model for them what I am teaching them regarding this. Help me to make you first, God, my spouse second, and my children third, and not to confuse these. Help me to model for my children what it looks like to incorporate these priorities in all I do daily, my work, my family life, and my relationships. If I have had blind spots in my own walk with You, Lord Jesus, please forgive me. Help me thirst for you like I do water on a parched summer day. I want to leave a kingdom-focused legacy, Lord, but I also just want to be closer to You for the sake of our relationship! I pray that my children see that, remember that, and desire that in their own lives too.

In Jesus Name, Amen.

CHAPTER 9

Sowing, Reaping, & Biblical Discipline

Obedience to God, His word, and His Spirit is rewarded with an indescribable sense of self-worth. There is something incredibly empowering about knowing you have done your very best at a task that God has called you to do for Him. But obedience isn't always easy. In fact, most of the time it requires sacrifice, courage, being stretched outside of comfort zones, and sometimes even suffering. Somtimes the sufferings we are called to endure are physical, and other times they are verbal persecutions that can attack our identity, intentions, or motives. Yes, sometimes obedience to God requires the sacrifice of our comfort, and usually it requires the sacrifice of our will.

As parents, we all have many hopes, dreams, and desires for our children. But if we were to pray for them to be obedient to the Lord, we would find that most of those hopes would be accomplished for His glory.

One of our most powerful prayer requests for our children is that they would be obedient to God alone. We can believe God that if our children are obedient to Him and seek Him and His Kingdom with their whole heart, soul, mind, and strength, all these things shall be given unto them. If our child is following Christ's lead and path, they will not stumble spiritually or be led astray.

So, how do we raise children to be obedient when they are older? It all starts with teaching them how to obey when they are younger, while they live in our homes under our leadership with accountability. The Bible instructs, "Children, obey your parents in the Lord, for this is right. "Honor your father and mother" (this is the first commandment with a promise),"that it may go well with you and that you may live long in the land." Eph. 6:1-3

> *"Children, obey your parents in all things: for this is well pleasing unto the Lord. Fathers, provoke not your children to anger, lest they be discouraged."*
>
> Colossians 3:20-21

We have an incredible responsibility in raising our children. We need to realize that as parents, we are image bearers of God to them. Their first thoughts, feelings, emotions, and impressions of God will be largely influenced by their earthly parents and, more specifically, their fathers. We do NOT want to give our children an impression of God that is derived from our irresponsible parenting by provoking them toward anger. If we develop a loving and reliable relationship with our child, where they can trust us and know of our deep loyalty and commitment to them, they should be *provoked by love* to obey us when we tell them to do something. On another note, we should have also developed a deep trust in our relationship with our child that cultivates an unwavering trust in us, so that they know we have their best interests in mind, so that they want to obey us out of a safe trust.

We need to realize that as parents, we are image bearers of God to them.

A lot of parents desire a quick fix to disobedience, but are unaware that it all begins with the relationship that they have built and are building with their child.

Even though your children love you, they will likely disobey you at some point because they are human and wrestle with the desires of the flesh like any of us. Selfishness, pride, and an independent spirit can affect all of us and sneak in when we least expect them. The question is, can we love God and still disobey him? Actually, the answer is that we can love God and struggle with sin, but disobedience to God is unloving. God doesn't want us to stay in bondage to our sin, and He died to set us free from it! As mature believers, Lord willing, we've learned to repent to God, and hopefully, you are at a place where you're not deliberately sinning against God in your life. But it's important to understand that our children are not born understanding this, so we must teach them using a biblical vocabulary.

Using your own life experiences as teaching examples, along with scriptural truth and a biblical vocabulary that teaches your children the foundational spiritual disciplines and gifts, such as confession, repentance, forgiveness, and grace, is essential to discipline and discipleship.

Discipline is one aspect of discipleship. Once we realize that it is in the moments that we encounter our child's sin as an opportunity for discipleship and leading them in true repentance to the cross to experience forgiveness and reconciliation with God and whomever they have offended, our entire perspective towards discipline changes.

I think one reason we see so many parents falling for wayward parenting philosophies is that they don't understand the incredible opportunity that is before them to be a minister of reconciliation! Too many parents take personal offense at their child's sin. Understandably so, as we have experienced that ourselves. But it's in those moments that parents must heed the warnings in scripture regarding their own reactions so they don't get tempted to sin as well.

Galatians 6:1-2 says, "Brothers, if anyone is caught in any transgression, you who are spiritual should restore him in a spirit of gentleness. Keep watch on yourself, lest you too be tempted. Bear one another's burdens, and so fulfill the law of Christ."

This scripture obviously applies to parents as we "catch our children in sin" at times. God's word is literally telling us how we should "restore" such a person. And then immediately, God's word says, "keep watch on yourself, lest you too be tempted" because He knows. God knows us so well and knows that when we are dealing with correcting someone's sin, there is inevitably a temptation for us to sin in confronting it.

Wow! This realization as a Mother changed everything for me. When Galatians 6:1-2 is coupled with Ephesians 6:4 and Colossians 3:21 above, where we are warned not to provoke our children to anger, wrath, or discouragement, I realized I have to be careful to check myself and if needed take a Mommy Timeout to calm down, pray, and make sure I am in a right space to deal with their sin so I don't sin more!

Therefore, we should never discipline our children in anger!

As parents, we must obey God's word to discipline our children, but we are also held accountable for how we do that.

You may be thinking of times in your parenting when you have failed and sinned against your children. That can be a heavy weight, one that can sometimes paralyze parents from obeying God's instructions in training our children up in the way. We encourage you not to allow your failures or mistakes to prevent you from obeying God in the future. All your sins were forgiven by Jesus on that cross. Own your sins, confess, repent, and move on forgiven. Realize the devil wants you to be disabled by condemning you for past sins, but in Jesus, you are free.

God has chosen you as your children's parents on purpose, and part of the reason is so that you train them in the way they should go, which includes correction. Children tend to repeat the same mistakes with their independent spirit, and if they are left uncorrected, you are, in essence, encouraging them to grow in this negative independent spirit that ignores authority, even though they love you.

This sounds like the issue with much of modern Christianity today, where people say they love Jesus, but they intentionally disobey Jesus with their lives. Resistance to God's authority later in life usually begins with disobedience to other authorities God has placed in our lives.

Jesus says, "If anyone loves me, he will keep my word, and my Father will love him, and we will come to him and make our home with him." John 14:23

You want your children to develop a heart for keeping Jesus' words, and that starts by fully expecting your children to obey your words. It will be a struggle for children to obey God if they cannot obey their own parents?.

Don't misunderstand, our children should not obey us to earn our love or prove their love for us. That is NOT what Jesus is saying here. He is saying that because of our great love for Him, we should want to obey His commands. Our love for Him provokes and motivates us to obey Him. Obedience is therefore a fruit of the relationship built, not a requirement for it.

Let's look at what scripture says about Sowing and Reaping for a moment:

> *"For the one who sows to his own flesh will from the flesh reap corruption, but the one who sows to the Spirit will from the Spirit reap eternal life."*
>
> Galatians 6:8

So there's a spiritual law that exists of sowing and reaping, and this scripture is talking about where someone ends up for eternity.

When your children are younger, they are largely protected from the more intense consequences of walking in the flesh. Unless you discipline them, they won't experience sowing and reaping in the same way as people do in their teenage years and adult lives.

We believe this is part of why it's so important to lovingly and biblically discipline your children when they are younger. Part of a parent's duty is to make sure they experience the spiritual law of sowing and reaping while they are growing up; otherwise, they won't learn the lesson until they are older, when the consequences are more severe and oftentimes hurt other people more deeply as well.

They must understand, with your help, the principle that all people will reap what they sow. That there are consequences for disobeying authority. That real love exhibits correction because love wants someone to live better.

The world has twisted the meaning of the word love into something that actually becomes the opposite of God's definition. There's no love apart from righteousness, but the world will influence that it's loving to let people live however they want and do whatever they want without consequence. That's not biblical love. That's moral relativism. That's what the world wants to pressure your children to adopt in the future.

Let's look at Psalm 85:10 for a moment:

> "Steadfast love and faithfulness meet; righteousness and peace kiss each other."

It's saying there isn't real love unless there's real faithfulness; love and faithfulness to God have to go together; likewise, righteousness and peace cannot exist without the other. There's only real peace in being reconciled to God through Jesus, who is holy, righteous, and just.

This is real love, and God calls us as parents to be peacemakers within our families. If we cannot do this well when children are younger, how in the world will we have peace in our families when they are older, and the family has grown?

Your children are demonstrating real love to you when they are obeying God and obeying you. Likewise, you are showing real

Resistance to God's authority later in life usually begins with unchecked disobedience to your authority in your home.

love to your children when you are correcting them because you are stepping into the gap as an ambassador for Christ and being activated in the ministry of reconciliation.

When you correct them biblically and consistently as they are growing up, you are cultivating in them a life of pursuing righteousness and experiencing the peace of knowing Jesus.

So shift your paradigm when your children disobey you from it being a nuisance or discouragement and start seeing it as an opportunity to correct them and point them to Jesus.

We cover the 10 steps to biblical discipline in the Parenting Mentor Program. You can learn more at courageousparenting.com.

Here is a short list of some of the most vital aspects of biblical discipline:

- Check yourself and never discipline in anger.
  "Brothers, if anyone is caught in any transgression, you who are spiritual should restore him in a spirit of gentleness. Keep watch on yourself, lest you too be tempted." Galatians 6:1
- Be clear to TEACH your children the expectations regarding sin, consequences, and punishment.
- Remind them they are disobeying God's word and use scripture to remind them.
- Decide on a method of correction that correlates with the situation and will also get the attention of your child, lead to discipleship, and reach the child of your heart.
  "The rod and reproof give wisdom, but a child left to himself brings shame to his mother." Prov. 29:15
  "Folly is bound up in the heart of a child, but the rod of discipline drives it far from him." Prov. 22:15
- Listen to their heart- encourage them to confess and apologize.
- Pray together, reconcile, don't withhold forgiveness, and guide them to repent and reconcile with God.

We often hear of parents who believe they are disciplining their children biblically and wonder why they aren't seeing a positive impact from it. If people are really honest, they will likely realize that either they aren't following through consistently or they aren't truly following what we have shared here. It's also possible that they gave up too early as well. Parenting is a long-game. It takes consistently following through over a long period of time before fruitfulness arrives.

GIVE VISION TO YOUR CHILDREN:

We need to teach our children that they have a massive impact on our culture NOW. They are a light to the world when they obey their parents and reflect the Spirit of God in how they respond to us. God gave them a powerful testimony by how they live! They get to show people that children are a blessing!

Teach your child today that God has a big purpose for them right now. And that they can shine a light for Jesus by obeying the Bible in being obedient to you, their parents. Reaffirm to them that you are on their team, want what is best for them, and would never ask them to do something that isn't good for them. Tell them that when you are telling them to clean their room or take care of a jurisdiction, it is because you love them and you want them to develop life skills, work ethic, and a heart that is trained in how to obey and steward the things God has given them well. It's about helping them to develop a character that God can trust! Share with your child about what God's word says about obedience and how you have to obey God even when you don't feel like it sometimes.

Likewise, parents, you also reflect God's image to the world by how you communicate, care for, love, disciple, and discipline your children. When we value our children and parent them in a way that is counter-cultural to the world, truly delighting in our children, you shine a bright light for Christ in this dark world in a way that can rattle even the most selfish of men and women.

Parenting QUESTIONS

- ❖ Do you struggle with provoking your children to anger or speaking in harsh tones to them?
- ❖ Have you discipled your children in what obedience is, understanding that it is a matter of the heart?
- ❖ Are you and your spouse in alignment regarding discipline in your home?
- ❖ Are you parenting as a team?
- ❖ Have you viewed correcting and disciplining in your home as an opportunity for discipleship and leading your child to Christ? How will this change your perspective in your home?

Share with your child about a time when it was difficult for you to obey God and how you needed the Holy Spirit to help you. What happened, and how did you feel after you disobeyed/obeyed? If you disobeyed, did you repent and change? What did that look like? Teach your child so that they know what it looks like.

Courageous Parenting CHALLENGE

- ❖ Teach your children three verses on obedience this week and pick one to memorize together. Recite it at every meal or in the car together.

Courageous Parenting PODCAST

- Don't Let Anger Destroy Your Home
- How to Overcome Anger in Your Parenting
- Why Your Kids Won't Obey You
- Discipling Your Children: The First Crucial Steps
- Bad Behavior is a Symptom of the Heart

PRAYER

Father God, we ask that You would help us, by the power of Your Holy Spirit, to model for our children what it looks like to be obedient to You. Help us to be vulnerable in sharing when You ask us to do things, how we struggle to be obedient, and what You are doing in our hearts. Help us to be consistent in training our children to be obedient and holding them accountable to Your Word. We pray that they will yield their hearts to Your will, Father. Guide our interactions with our children when we are correcting their disobedience. Help us to have long suffering, patience, and forbearance with our children, and to remember that we are your ambassadors and are reflecting You to them. Help us to be thoughtful and loving in our correction, but to be consistent and clear, always bringing them back to Your holy Word. May our children love You and obey You above all else, Lord, and follow Your lead throughout their lives. Protect our minds and hearts from being deceived by worldly parenting philosophies and keep our eyes on You, Jesus. I ask Your Holy Spirit to give us wisdom in our parenting. Guide us, forgive us when we mess up, and help us to be humble and ask our children for forgiveness. God, would You grant us grace and mercy and help us not to be too hard on ourselves because we know we are not perfect and will need more of Your grace in the future. Thank you for laying your life down so that we might be forgiven.

In Jesus' Name, Amen.

CHAPTER 10

Humility & The Benefits of Biblical Community

One of the most vital skills a Christian can gain is the ability to put aside the innate desire of humanity to justify wrongdoing and self-preserve, but instead to be truthful about fleshly desires, temptations, faults, sins, and shortcomings.

Jesus Himself asked the Jewish leaders to examine themselves when he was advocating for the adulterous woman: "Let him who is without sin among you be the first to throw a stone at her." John 8:7

One of the greatest sins is justifying and rationalizing sin, which often then leads to blame shifting. This self-preserving instinct is, in fact, the first act of sin we can witness in our children when they deny that the wrongdoing is sin or even their fault. It also happens to be exactly how our ancestors reacted to being caught in sin for the first time in the Garden of Eden, when we witness both Adam and Eve blame shifting when God holds them accountable. (Genesis 2-3)

We all struggle with sin in this world. Still, those of us who are unable to recognize, confess, and repent of sin humbly are at risk of habitual sin, which entangles and entraps the Christian, disabling them from fully experiencing freedom in Christ. The habitual sin then becomes a bondage that affects relationships with other people and ultimately their relationship with God.

First, we need to teach our children the truth about sin and the struggle of the human flesh with which we reside while here on earth.

> *"If we say we have no sin, we deceive ourselves, and the truth is not in us."*
>
> 1 John 1:8

Then we need to model for our children what it looks like to be introspective and then sincerely confess and repent of sins. "If we confess our sins, He is faithful and just to forgive us our sins and to cleanse us from all unrighteousness." 1 John 1:9

How can our children experience freedom from the bondage of sin if they don't have the habit of being introspective and the humility to repent? The answer is that they can't.

One outward expression of humility and self-examination is remorse.

Being able to look at oneself objectively will make or break many relationships in his/her life and is one of the most fundamental skills you can train in your child. It will impact their marriage, family, friendships, relationships within the Body of Christ, as well as work relationships. Being able to view oneself rightly, in the light of the cross, helps us not only to admit when we have wronged someone but also to offer forgiveness to others when they have been offended.

When we see our sin, we can have compassion for others and offer them the same grace we would hope for and have been given through Jesus Christ, our Lord.

Being introspective is identified most often, like the ability to label one's sins and heart attitudes, but it also causes remembrance of past pain, motivating compassion, mercy, and even forgiveness.

One outward expression of humility and self-examination is remorse.

These two factors go hand in hand. Can you imagine someone with the ability to label others' sins and heart attitudes who is unable to be introspective? They would most likely be continually pointing out the error in others without recognizing the beam or log in their own eye. Consider the alternative, someone who is reflective but unable to label the root of the issue. This poor soul would probably be chronically hard on themselves while never fully experiencing triumph or victory over their sins. Instead, they might stay stuck in the same rut for years, trapped and without hope.

Besides, God desires for us to be in a restored relationship with one another, which isn't possible without both introspection and the ability to label what we are asking forgiveness for.

> *"Why do you see the speck that is in your brother's eye, but do not notice the log that is in your own eye? Or how can you say to your brother, 'Let me take the speck out of your eye,' when there is the log in your own eye? You hypocrite, first take the log out of your own eye, and then you will see clearly to take the speck out of your brother's eye."*
>
> Matthew 7:3-5

You see, the Lord wants us to be able to speak truth in love and be ambassadors of Him, literally partnering with Christ in the ministry of reconciliation! But we cannot do that when we have sin in our lives! We cannot correct someone of a sin or help them out if we still struggle with the same sin. We cannot operate with one eye!

God's word exhorts all Christians to examine themselves and get right with God so that we can actually do the ministry He has created us for, which is to be ministers of reconciliation! In 2 Cor. 5:17-21, "Therefore, if anyone is in Christ, he is a new creation. The old has passed away; behold, the new has come. All this is from God, who through Christ reconciled us to himself and gave us the ministry of reconciliation; that is, in Christ God was reconciling the world to himself, not counting their trespasses against them, and entrusting to us the message of reconciliation. Therefore, we are ambassadors for Christ, God making his appeal through us. We implore you on behalf of Christ, be reconciled to God. For our sake, he made him to be sin who knew no sin, so that in him we might become the righteousness of God."

Parenting QUESTIONS

- Does your child witness you being introspective and humbly apologizing for specific heart attitudes and sins? Your children will more likely learn and mimic the behaviors they see in you than what you verbally teach them.
- Do you hold your child accountable by speaking truth into their life, pointing out their sins, and giving consequences for those sins?
- Do you allow your child to say, "sorry," without genuine remorse? Have you taught them different heart attitudes to be on the lookout for in their hearts, and have you expected them to be more sincere with their apologies?
- Have your children witnessed you confess and repent of sin? Do they know these biblical words? If not, take time to teach them! We must parent using a biblical vocabulary.

Here are two common examples:

Your three-year-old is struggling to share and steals a toy from another child. Do you usher them over to say "sorry," or do you teach them what to say and enforce them being clear about what they did? "I am sorry for not sharing and being selfish with the toy. Do you teach them what repentance means, to turn away from and not do it again? One recommendation would be to encourage them to verbalize that they won't do that again and ask for forgiveness.

If your child is the offended one, do you focus on teaching forgiveness and making sure they are not allowing a bitter root to grow?

Your fourteen-year-old was told to pick up her room. You go into her room to inspect and find that she hasn't followed through. Does she sassily say, "Sorry," and then continue scrolling through her phone? Or does she say, "I am sorry I didn't listen and obey you the first time, Mom, that was disrespectful? I will work on it now."

Way before your child is fourteen years old, they should have learned to be introspective, know what they did wrong, and offer a sincere apology. But of course it's never too late.

Courageous Parenting CHALLENGE

❖ If you have not modeled for your child what this discipline of self-examination, humility, and repentance looks like, go and apologize to your child. If you have struggled with being prideful or lording over your children, you need to confess that to them and repent to God, asking Him to help you change.

Courageous Parenting PODCAST

- How to Prevent Your Past from Hurting Your Parenting (Ep. 55)[5]
- Spiritual Spring Cleaning in the Hearts of Your Home (Ep. 394)[6]

PRAYER

Father, we want to grow in our relationship with you, and we want that for our children as well. We know that sin prevents communion with you and others, and we don't want to let anything stand in our way of experiencing the joys and blessings of Biblical relationships. Help us to be humble and admit when we are in sin. Help us to fully forgive those who offend us. Will You help us in teaching our children how to diagnose their sins so that we can have victory over them and work towards living in your freedom!? We don't want pride to hold our children or us back anymore. And we want our children to experience the full blessing in their relationships as they grow. Help us to teach our children, hold them accountable, and model for them what it should look like to be humble and readily admit.

In Jesus Christ's Name and For His Glory We Pray, Amen.

CHAPTER 11

Vital Listening Skills

You've said those phrases a million times, "Are you listening to me?" "Look at me in the eyes!" and "What did I just say?"

Listening is one of the most essential skills we can equip our children with. It will undoubtedly impact every relationship they will ever encounter. Yet Moms and Dads alike are regularly commiserating, describing the age-old parenting struggle of getting their children actually to hear them.

Do you ever feel like you're preaching to a wall, like your words are just going in and coming out, or maybe they aren't even making it into your child's consciousness?

Moms grow weary and get discouraged while desiring to stay consistent in the training of their younger children when they don't feel they are making progress.

Parents of teenagers often complain of disrespect and fear that they have lost their child's hearts entirely. Some recount the sharp words that pierce their soul, "I HATE YOU," as the slamming of the door vibrates in their memory. And others share a tragic phase they describe as the silent treatment.

Regardless of your child's age, there is a desperate need for us parents to wake up and teach our children how to communicate healthily! If we want our children to have marriages that last, healthy relationships with their siblings and us, connect with their children, or have a powerful witness in this world, we must teach them how to listen and hear people.

Most relational issues stem from communication. If we can equip our children with superb listening skills, then they will be much more prepared for their future.

As God's ambassadors, the goal of our every action, including communication, should be to glorify Him and make Him known as the great God He is. In our everyday conversations and nonverbal communication, we are to show people the fruits of the Spirit: love, joy, peace, patience, kindness, goodness, faithfulness, gentleness, and self-control.

Here are four things you can do to teach your child how to be a good listener:

1. Lead by example. Are you a good listener? You may think you are, but what do others think? What do those closest to you think? Ask them. We cannot teach and expect our children to implement what we cannot model. Model good listening and communication skills.
2. Teach your children WHY being a good listener is important! This skill will be vital to their success in relationships for the rest of their lives, in family, business, friendship, and especially in their relationship with the Lord.
3. Train your children to have self-control and discernment in when to speak; teach them to care about the other person's needs and the goal of every conversation (this also requires training in humility and respect for others).
4. Don't overpromise and always follow through so that your words stay meaningful to your children.

> *"Let what you say be simply 'Yes' or 'No'; anything more than this comes from evil."*
>
> Mt 5:37

We have to be careful not to do too much talking as it can lead to exaggerated consequences we won't follow through on, over-promising in the moment to create compliance, or disrespect because our words over time lose integrity.

When parents are in a moment of pressure, we can say things we don't mean, and in those moments, our words just become noise and lessen the power of the original "no" or "yes" as well.

Is your word as good as gold to your children? If it is, you will become more thoughtful about consequences and rarely make promises, because you understand how vital it is that we follow through on everything we say. The more integrous your words are, the less you will need to use them and the more impactful they will be over time. That being said, with very small children, you may not see a difference in this, but you certainly will as they get older.

How many times have you gotten down on your knees, held your young child's hands, and said, "Look at mommy (or daddy) in the eyes, to get their attention?

From the time our children are responding to us as babies, we all have an excellent opportunity to teach the value of listening.

It starts the minute we take the time to lock eyes with our precious babies as they are looking up at us in between snuggles. Teaching our child to listen begins with how we model listening to them. And then how we model listening to our spouse and other children.

Sometimes it's important to give respect even when they don't deserve it, and you'll see them rise to it.

If you have a teenager, lead them in how to respect by overwhelming them with the same respect you expect from them.

Here's a counterintuitive leadership tip for teenagers: Sometimes it's important to give respect even when they don't deserve it, and you'll see them rise to it.

It's that simple. Children want to be heard and are trying to figure out how to process their feelings, emotions, thoughts, and knowledge, and they're profoundly curious. Children are always learning, and they need a safe place to process.

If you are always correcting your child and never letting them come up with self-inspired ideas or allowing them the time to grow on their journey towards getting wisdom, you will be paralyzing your relationship as well as their development.

Angie shares a regretful mistake she made in parenting:

> Listen, I get it. The reason I am sharing this with you is that I have failed at this majorly as a Mom. I have overwhelmed four and fifteen-year-olds with forty-five-minute and two-hour lectures because I was so deeply concerned. I submerged them in the Word, diving deep into Scripture and digging in for far too long, which could have potentially left them despising the Word. Thankfully, it didn't discourage our children from loving God's word.

I could easily be accused and found guilty of doing this many times. This is one area Motherhood has been sanctifying in me.

Now, sometimes, a forty-five-minute talk is necessary, but where I went wrong was that I did most of the talking and not enough listening. Don't make the same mistake I did. Instead, choose to show the respect you so desire from your child. Ask questions, hear from their heart, let the Spirit lead when you speak, and then get on your knees and take it to the one who can change a child's heart.

> *"Know this, my beloved brothers: let every person be quick to hear, slow to speak, slow to anger;"*
>
> James 1:19

Listening skills are vital to grow in strong discernment as well. In a future where it's hard to decipher what's real or not online, where it's difficult to know for sure where information is coming from, it will take a person with heightened awareness to be able to discern what to actually allow to influence them.

This awareness starts from growing as a patient and proactive listener with people. Paying attention to all the signals, whether in person or online, to decipher what's really happening, what's not being said, catching manipulation, deception, and preventing unwise choices.

Parenting QUESTIONS

- Have you been good at listening in the moments of discipline, or do you struggle with impatience and bulldozing with your words?
- Are your children good listeners, or do they tend to struggle to talk over others, interrupt, and rudely insist on their own way?
- Do your children tend to struggle with anger outbursts when in conflict with others? Are they good at listening?

Courageous Parenting CHALLENGE

- Take time to listen to your child without giving advice or teaching. Take time to just know your child, be in their presence, and offer them the opportunity to talk and share their heart.

Courageous Parenting PODCAST

- Leading the Attitudes in Your Home (Ep. 255)

PRAYER:

Father, thank you for always being there for us when we need someone to listen; for the wise counsel Your Word provides, and for giving us Your divine power in the Holy Spirit to be able to exercise self-control and LISTEN. Help us show what a good listener looks like to our children. Would you intervene in our relationships, allowing us parents to have the influence you want us to have in our children's lives? Help us to lead well and to connect with our children. Help us to be good examples of being respectful, making eye contact, and valuing our children. Help our children to know how much we love them and want to hear their thoughts. Might we bring You glory, equipping them with tools like listening skills so that they can fulfill the purposes You have created them for in their relationships?

In Jesus' Name, Amen.

CHAPTER 12

How to Cultivate a Teachable Heart

Do your children love you? Most parents will agree that this is true. However, this doesn't mean you have their hearts. In fact, as children get older, most parents actually lose their children's hearts, while their children absolutely still love them.

This is an important distinction to make because it has to do with your influence. If you lose influence, you can't guide them. One of the biggest warnings we received when we were young, with a growing family, was to stop having children because the teenage years were falsely prophesied to be so hard.

It came out with a sharp, doubtful phrase to discourage us from growing our family.

"Just wait until the teenage years…"

Instead of believing the lie, we became even more thoughtful and asked the Lord for wisdom in how we could experience something different from what most were testifying to by changing what we were doing in the present.

If you want different outcomes than the masses, you have to be willing to consistently do things differently than most people.

How do we keep their hearts in the teenage years? How do we stay the most important influences in their lives, in their eyes? How do we make sure our words carry weight and cause consideration?

If you want different outcomes than the masses, you have to be willing to consistently do things differently than most people.

This topic itself could be a whole book; perhaps we will write it one day!

It starts with caring about their heart condition and becoming good at diagnosing where their heart is. You'll never work to correct and influence change if you don't know at the core, the problem that exists.

Heart attitudes are one of the most important conditions for a parent to diagnose, yet one of the hardest things to accurately label at times.

Here is a list of a few sinful attitudes you might have seen in your children:

- Pride
- Selfishness
- Jealousy or Covetousness
- Contempt
- Anger
- Vengeful (Desiring Revenge)
- Unforgiving Heart Attitude
- Disobedient
- Defiant or Disrespectful
- Manipulative
- Self-preserving
- Grumbling or Complaining

It's equally important that we use a biblical vocabulary in affirming and calling out the godly/righteous character qualities we desire and want to encourage in our children as well. One of the most important warnings we tell parents is this: If you only focus on the sins and on correcting in your home, you will likely not enjoy or delight in your children, in fact, you might find that you start to truly grow weary, discouraged, and even discontent and be tempted to covet, become jealous, or desire to delegate the raising of your children to someone else so you can escape the realities of the condition of the hearts in your home. Not only will delighting in your children be difficult, but your children will also become discouraged and possibly even develop a crushed spirit. It is vital that as biblical parents we recognize the importance of both being consistent in training our children in the instruction and admonition of the Lord while also understanding the incredible power of the tongue and that God warns us that it has the power to speak life or death, to set a blaze a fire, and to bless and curse. We have to make a purposeful effort to exercise self-control, but also to train ourselves in speaking life and learning when to be slow to speak, waiting on the prompting of the Spirit.

Here is a list of godly character qualities we can be on the lookout for, encourage, and affirm our children in, and call them up to!

- Respectful
- Teachable Heart
- Compassionate
- Merciful
- Thankful
- Grateful
- Servant Hearted
- Gentle
- Joyful
- Obedient
- Graceful
- Forgiving

Being able to label and see what heart attitudes your child has in their character is essential in knowing what we need to train or focus on with our children. It's encouraging when you can identify and verbally acknowledge positive character qualities you see in your child as well.

As parents, we must be careful to make an equal effort in diagnosing the sinful heart attitudes as we do in acknowledging the godly character qualities our children have already gained.

Of all the heart attitudes, cultivating a teachable heart in your child and developing a relationship with them where you are their foremost teacher, counselor, and confidant is crucial in raising up the next generation. Without a teachable heart attitude, you can kiss equipping your children for unprecedented times goodbye.

Implementing what's in this book will help you cultivate a teachable heart in your children, but like everything else, you cannot teach your children to be something you are not. You must model for them what a lifelong learner looks like. If you have a teachable heart, it is much easier to train your children to also have one. If you are prideful and struggle with thinking you know it all, well, the apple will likely not fall far from the tree.

Parenting QUESTIONS

- Do you have a teachable heart attitude? Do your children see it?
- On a scale of 1-5, one being not at all and five being all the time, how would you rate yourself at labeling heart attitudes and praying for your children, specifically using a biblical vocabulary?
- Labeling and holding our children accountable for and affirming their heart attitudes should be a regular part of daily conversations with them. How often do you point out the excellent heart attitudes you see in your child? How often do you hold them accountable for their sinful heart attitudes?
- How do you think this one change could stimulate more in-depth conversations with your children?

Courageous Parenting CHALLENGE

- Of the list above, which heart attitudes do you see in each of your children? Remember that we cannot change other people, but we CAN pray for them and influence them. Write down each of your children's names and write out a prayer for each of them.

Courageous Parenting PODCAST

- Cultivating a Teachable Heart (Ep. 193)

PRAYER

Father, we know You care genuinely for our hearts. You blessed us with the gift of relationship for many reasons; one was so that we could grow, that through conflict, our sins would come to light, and we would be made more like Your Son as we pursue righteousness and rid ourselves of all uncleanliness. Help us have gentle tongues as we rebuke and hold our children accountable. Might they receive both the hard-to-hear diagnosis as well as the praiseworthy acknowledgments? Help us look for both the good and the evil that is bound up in the heart of my child so that we might obey Your Word and train them up in the way they should go. Thank You for giving us Your Holy Spirit so that we could experience Your power, conquering the things that hold us back. Might our children and we experience the fruits of the Spirit! We pray this in the name of Your Son, Jesus, Amen.

CHAPTER 13

Equipped to Discern Influences Biblically

We live in a fallen world, and that reality should cause us to view the current state of culture and society through a realistic lens that leads to an understanding that it is vital, more now than ever, that our children know how to influence their environments and lead their peers. The first step is to empower your children with the understanding of what influence is, and secondly, to recognize the depravity of humankind.

It is crucial that children understand the power of influence and that they decide whether to be followers or leaders.

Real-Life Example of How to Teach it:

We were driving our children to church one Sunday morning, and Isaac began the discussion about influence, what it was, its power, and why they have to be wise concerning who and what they allow to influence them. We told our children to discern/judge who is worthy to influence them and be guarded when it comes to who they follow. Yes, we encouraged them to judge. Many say they don't want their children to be judgmental, but what they really mean is that they don't want them to have a critical spirit and be unloving. We should want our children to judge. In fact, we should teach them HOW to judge and make wise decisions.

We must also teach our children to be full of grace and compassion, mindful of their own sin, and to know that everyone is on their own spiritual journey. However, none of us may tolerate blatant sin and allow our brothers and sisters in Christ to remain enslaved by it. And we most definitely don't want our children to be influenced by those who are unrepentant.

Parenting QUESTIONS

- ❖ Do you know who is influencing your child?
- ❖ How much weight do your words carry with your children? Do they question you?
- ❖ Do your children want your advice? Do they respect you? Do you show your children respect?

As parents, we can easily lower our ability to influence by living hypocritically. Make sure you are not a parent who lives by the saying, "Do as I say, not as I do."

You have the right as a parent to choose who has influence in your child's life. When your children are young, you choose who their friends and influences are. As they get older, teach them what Scripture says about choosing friends wisely. Whom are your children's hearts knitted toward? Is it you or is it becoming stronger towards a coach, a teacher, an uncle, or a babysitter?

Make sure you are not a parent who lives by the saying, "Do as I say, not as I do."

Courageous Parenting CHALLENGE

- ❖ Look up these Scriptures to further study what God's Word instructs us regarding judging.
  - Read Matthew 7:1-2

    - Is it the judging that Jesus is warning against or the heart attitude behind the judging?
- ❖ Christians often judge people outside of the church, yet they don't judge those inside. Did you know that's the opposite of what the bible says?
    - James 2:12-13
    - Read 1 Corinthians 5:12-13
    - What virtue/character quality are we to judge with?

*These are only a few of the many verses on judging found in the Bible. We recommend doing a word study and looking up EVERY Bible verse on this topic and writing it down. Ask God to give you understanding as you study His Word, and then teach your children what the Bible says.

Give us courage and perseverance to parent according to your Word, not the World.

If your children are mature enough, open up a discussion about judging, influences, and discernment. Ask them what they think of those words, what they mean, and then teach them about what the Bible says, how the Bible is our guidebook for life, our manual, and how we need to be careful not to judge souls, but also that God does want us to use discernment and make wise choices. Use this conversation as an opportunity to talk to your children about influences in their own lives and challenge them to be leaders.

Remember that without judging, nobody would be held accountable, no student would ever be graded, and no one would ever forgive. The truth is, we need to teach our children how to judge wisely, righteously, actually. They need to judge which foods and movies are healthy and unhealthy just as they need to judge which friends are healthy and unhealthy.

Courageous Parenting PODCAST

- Teaching Your Kids the Power of Influences (Ep. 173)
- Equipping Kids to Handle Bad Peer Influences (Ep. 281)
- How to Influence the Influencers in Your Child's Life (Ep. 264)
- Helping Kids Discern What is True in a Disinformation World (Ep. 181)

PRAYER

Father, Christians today have been deceived into believing that they are not to judge others because that's what is taught in the majority of Christian circles. While Your word warns us that "with the judgment you pronounce you will be judged, and with the measure you use it will be measured to you" in Matthew 7:2, we also know that You call us to discern between good and evil and not to be deceived. God, give our children the wisdom to know when to judge and the boldness to stand firm in truth and expose evil. Protect them from the evil works of darkness and guard their hearts from growing cold in love towards others. Many of us have neglected our parental duty to protect our children from certain influences because we are so pressured to be "tolerant." Please redeem our mistakes and help us be courageous, living out what your Word says, raising our children in the way they should go. Give us the courage to guide them down the right path and to confidently warn our children when they start heading down a wrong or sinful path. Parenting is hard, Lord. And this aspect of it is especially difficult. Give us courage and perseverance to parent according to your Word, not the World.

In Jesus' Name, Amen.

CHAPTER 14

Prepared to Navigate Friendships Biblically

Peers have a lot of influence on a child's life. Every human has this innate desire to be liked, loved, and to feel like they belong. These desires can largely influence children in the friend choices they make, so it is vital to teach your children how to choose friends wisely.

While parents are largely in charge of choosing their small children's friends based upon the families they choose to be in community with, the reality is that the older your children get, the more activities they join, and it will become increasingly important to have taught your children some basics regarding choosing friends wisely.

We have taught our children that it's important to be *friendly* to everyone, as Christ's ambassador, but that it's ok to have a few close friends and be wise about who those are.

The Word is full of warnings and guidance regarding choosing friends wisely.

"Do not be deceived: 'Bad company ruins good morals.'" 1 Cor. 15:33

"One who is righteous is a guide to his neighbor, but the way of the wicked leads them astray." Proverbs 12:26

"Whoever walks with the wise becomes wise, but the companion of fools will suffer harm." Proverbs 13:20

"Make no friendship with a man given to anger, nor go with a wrathful man, lest you learn his ways and entangle yourself in a snare." Proverbs 22:24-25

God's Word also has wisdom as far as what to look for in a friend: "Greater love has no one than this, that someone lay down his life for his friends." John 15:13

"Iron sharpens iron, and one man sharpens another." Proverbs 27:17

"Two are better than one, because they have a good reward for their toil. For if they fall, one will lift up his fellow. But woe to him who is alone when he falls and has not another to lift him up!" Ecc. 4:9-10

"Bear one another's burdens, and so fulfill the law of Christ." Gal. 6:2

"Rejoice with those who rejoice, weep with those who weep." Romans 12:15

These are all great descriptions of the kind of qualities we should teach our children to look for and pray for in their friends. We should teach our children to be aware of the symptoms of a dangerous friend and what characteristics a good friend ought to have. Our children need to be careful in whom they confide. Their discernment of who is trustworthy and who is not is critical.

Questions to ask your child about their friends:

- Are they Christians, and do they desire to grow in the Lord?
- Do they gossip? (They will most likely gossip about you.)
- Can they rejoice with you when you have something to celebrate? Or are they jealous?
- Can they weep with you and give you space to grieve?
- Are they like-minded biblically?
- Will they challenge and encourage you to grow in God?
- Will they speak the truth, hold you accountable, and call out sin in your life?
- Are they forgiving and compassionate?
- Do they confess and repent of their sin? (humility)
- Are they living in habitual unrepentant sin?

The friends your children choose will undoubtedly influence your child. When your children are young, you have the jurisdiction and right to choose who your child spends time with. Yes, I am advocating for you, the parent, to help your child choose his/her friends. As they get older, remind them of these questions and teach them to be wary of bad qualities in others.

As you teach your children about these qualities, challenge them to be a good friend, but remind them that they need to work on the relationships in their family first.

One thing we have always said to our children is that they need to "get their relationships right at home first." What we mean by that is that they don't get the privilege of hanging out with friends if they are on bad terms with a sibling. What they are showing me is their friendship skills, or lack thereof. If we don't believe they are giving their best to the family, then they are not allowed to spend time with their other friends.

As your child spends time with other children, be watchful for attitude changes, opinions, and belief changes. If your child is weak and allows the other children to lead them, it's time to step in and have another lesson on being a leader, not a follower.

Parenting QUESTIONS

- Do you have friendships that model biblical community?
- Have you spent any time teaching your children about how to choose wise friends?
- How do you feel you are cultivating lifelong friendships between your children? Be careful not to allow friends to become an idol in your child's life.
- Have you allowed friendships to come in between siblings? If so, how can you help encourage healing and closer sibling relationships?

Courageous Parenting CHALLENGE

- ❖ If you have been hanging out with questionable friends at the expense of spending time with more like-minded people, make wiser choices. Be intentional with people who will challenge you to grow in God and whose children have godly character qualities that you admire and want to see in your children. Don't ever sacrifice the health, growth, and safety of your family for the sake of relationships with those who are not pursuing Christ.

Courageous Parenting PODCAST

- Equipping Kids to Handle Bad Peer Influences
- Cultivating Strong Sibling Relationships
- Don't Let Anyone Confuse Your Children

PRAYER

Lord, we know that no one is perfect, but we also don't want to be foolish by choosing unwise company. Help us to make wise decisions in who we invest time into relationally and teach our children how to be purposeful in building biblical community. Give us eyes to see and courage to discern truth and make hard decisions for the sake of protecting our family. Lord, let us be a light and hold to the truth found in your Word. We pray for our children to make wise choices in life and to select friendships with those who are like-minded over those who are popular or pursuing them. Guide them, give them wisdom and understanding about how they will become like those they hang out with. Help them to be wise in who they allow to influence them and who they invest in leading. Help them to see the difference. Holy Spirit, please place a desire in my child's heart for a friend that will be as iron sharpens iron. We pray they grow in discernment and have the courage to speak truth in love when they are faced with adversity. We also ask you to truly implant in our children a heart of compassion, understanding, and grace for those who need You, Lord. Might they become agents of change, Ambassadors for Christ who are willing to stand in the gap and witness to those who are lost?

For Christ's Glory and Sake, Amen.

CHAPTER 15

Protect, Preserve, & Equip for Purity

In today's society, the word purity seems like a taboo topic. The moment you mention Christian concepts like modesty, purity, protecting or preserving innocence, you are likely to have naysayers and cancel culture activists persecuting you and even accusing you of being involved in certain movements that frankly also went extreme in the ditch of control and legalism. Over the last 25 years in our parenting journey, we have observed the pendulum swing from one extreme to another in different Christian circles, both missing the mark biblically and both harmful. Many Christians and even pastors will not touch this topic with a ten-foot pole because it's so controversial.

On one hand, you have extreme purists, who in some cases may have had pure intentions with the motive to protect their wives and children, while others have crossed the line, lording over the women in their families in an attempt to control and even impress upon them unfairly the full burden of responsibility for others' sin, or lack of self-control, which is wrong. On the other side of the spectrum, in another ditch, you will easily find the purity cancel culture, with their personal testimonies of trauma, which are legitimate and traumatizing, but influencing others not to teach purity at all, even implying that to teach purity is a form of abuse. So while one side is supposed to lead to purity, but has produced mixed fruit of hurt and purity, the other side is promoting sexual liberty, exploration, and not teaching purity at all. But like any spectrum, you have a myriad of beliefs and convictions that fall all in between. Regardless of where you land on the spectrum as Christ-followers, we should desire to live in His will for our lives, not from a works-based theology, but rather a grace-based theology filled with love for a Holy God!

The problem arises when people solely base their convictions on this topic on others' personal experiences and viewpoints rather than simply going to the Word of God. This is where we would caution any parent.

Regardless of what your experience was as a child, or what documentaries you have watched, or people you have followed and been influenced by online, if you are pursuing to live biblically and be a biblical parent, you cannot dismiss that God wants his people to be set apart and to pursue purity since it is written, "You shall be holy, for I am holy." 1 Peter 1:16

We know that sexual sin hurts, but God redeems and heals all brokenness.

As parents, we should not be ashamed to want the best for our children. We wouldn't give our children contaminated water on purpose. We want what is best for our children, so why wouldn't we want them to have less sin, pain, and temptation for bondage? We should thirst for what is pure and holy and desire our children to crave the same thing because it's God's will for us.

There are many scriptures that talk about sexual sin, urging the Christian to walk by the Spirit and not by the flesh, but one thing we believe is missed altogether is that God calls us to more than being physically sexually pure. He wants all of us; our heart, soul, mind, and strength (physical).

Matthew 22:37-39 says, "You shall love the Lord your God with all your heart and with all your soul and with all your mind. This is the great and first commandment. And a second is like it: You shall love your neighbor as yourself."

You cannot love your neighbor as God desires if you are not loving God with all you are first. Sexual sin oftentimes doesn't only hurt you, but also "your neighbor" as well as your relationship with God because all sin separates us from God. Thankfully, we can experience regeneration and forgiveness of all our sins because of what Christ did on the cross for us, but it does require genuine repentance.

The reality is that there are those who have experienced trauma, hurt, and are in need of healing who were raised in both kinds of cultures; those hyper-focused on sexual purity, as well as those where there was no standard, teaching, or protection. The one undeniable truth is that we live in a fallen world and sin is rampant, humanity is depraved, and sin exists everywhere humans are to a certain degree. But, we don't change God's word to fit our world and throw the baby out with the bath water, so to speak, by lowering our standards. We are called to protect our children in every way we can!

Instead, we must teach what is biblical, true, and most healthy, but be vigilant to be most concerned with the souls of our children! We must teach our children to follow the instructions in God's Word regarding purity, regardless of what the culture, even some so-called Christian cultures, deem acceptable. And when you experience adversity, go back to the Word of God and wrestle with the truth. Part of following Christ is learning to lay down your cross and take up His. Being willing to be different from the world and be a light!

As parents wanting to protect our children and raise them biblically, we had our personal boundaries, which we quickly found are never going to perfectly align with anyone else's. Let's take the topic of modesty, for example, it is a vague term with a spectrum of beliefs and convictions; each family needs to define it clearly with their children, both sons and daughters. Teaching your children that you want to protect them for their good but that others may have different convictions or none at all on the topic simply because they have not studied it and that above all else as Christians we don't want to cause division on the topic but be loving towards all people is so important, because you may land in one place in your decision regarding modesty and realize there are others who are more conservative than you and others who are less. That realization is humbling, that many could interpret a topic like modesty so differently. And while there are many topics like this among the churches, the important realization is that these are the disputable issues that really have nothing to do with our salvation since we are saved by faith in Christ alone and not by our works or outward appearance. Nonetheless, the topic of modesty is one that is important for couples to discuss and be in alignment as they are raising their children.

So what does one do in a position of disagreement in a marriage? Go to Romans Chapter 14: 1-12: "As for the one who is weak in faith, welcome him, but not to quarrel over opinions. One person believes he may eat anything, while the weak person eats only vegetables. Let not the one who eats despise the one who abstains, and let not the one who abstains pass judgment on the one who eats, for God has welcomed him. Who are you to pass judgment on the servant of another? It is before his own master that he stands or falls. And he will be upheld, for the Lord is able to make him stand.

One person esteems one day as better than another, while another esteems all days alike. Each one should be fully convinced in his own mind. The one who observes the day observes it in honor of the Lord. The one who eats, eats in honor of the Lord, since he gives thanks to God, while the one who abstains, abstains in honor of the Lord and gives thanks to God. For none of us lives to himself, and none of us dies to himself. For if we live, we live to the Lord, and if we die, we die to the Lord. So then, whether we live or whether we die, we are the Lord's. For this end Christ died and lived again, that he might be Lord both of the dead and of the living.

Why do you pass judgment on your brother? Or you, why do you despise your brother? For we will all stand before the judgment seat of God; for it is written,

> "As I live, says the Lord, every knee shall bow to me, and every tongue shall confess to God."

So then each of us will give an account of himself to God."

This scripture leads us to recommend that within a marriage, the head of household needs to lead in a loving way, recognizing that the one with a convicted conscience needs to be honored and loved, not being tempted to sin. If going with the more liberal opinion causes the conservative one to sin, that is tempting one to stumble. Regardless of who holds the more liberal view of the issue, this scripture is exhorting us to bear with one another these issues in a selfless, loving way, counting others as more important than ourselves.

The whole point is that God cares most about the heart.

God created our mind, body, soul, and heart, which includes our emotions; all interconnected. It is vital, as we discuss purity, that we understand the need for teaching our children how to protect their purity in all of these areas, not just in the physical sense. As parents, we will be held accountable by God for protecting the purity of our children as well as how we train them while they are under our jurisdiction. Because our children will not always be under our jurisdiction, we must help them to develop their own conviction regarding purity and teach them how they can guard their minds, hearts, souls, and bodies against the temptation to sin. They will need to be intentional about setting boundaries in friendships and being wise, so they do not find themselves in precarious and dangerous situations that cost them their purity and steal their mental and spiritual innocence.

Some well-intentioned parents warn their children against premarital sex, but neglect to also have a standard of purity of mind. We teach our children how to guard their minds by setting boundaries that will shield their eyes, the entry point for addiction to sexual sin for so many today. But for our children to adopt the conviction to guard their own eyes when they are older, they must be taught why.

Courageous parents are willing to set boundaries that are counter-cultural, but they don't just leave it there. They go the next step to disciple their children in what Scripture says about guarding our minds and hearts in Christ Jesus. Technology is producing sexual temptations we never had to battle against when we were their age, but

God's Word has relevant scriptures that speak to this temptation of sin. Equip your children by helping them to have these verses written on their hearts.

This is an area that takes more courage than most parents are willing to put forward, because your decisions will look different from those in the Church. We have assembled a list of good discussion topics for couples to discuss that will potentially help parents protect the purity of their children. Remember, the goal is NOT to be in alignment with us and our choices, but instead to pursue alignment in your marriage and make decisions as parents that first align with scripture. The hardest part is that while the Bible does talk about purity and being proactive to protect it and make biblical choices, it doesn't say exactly how to go about it in every circumstance. For example, the bible does not discuss sleepovers. You, as a parent, have to evaluate all other scriptures regarding parenting, testing the spirits, discerning good from evil, and judging appropriately to make the wisest decision for your child's safety! That may look slightly different from family to family, based on whether the family is also biblically like-minded or not, for example!

- What are the boundaries you are teaching your children to set regarding other people's devices? We tell our children to never look at another child's device, even if they ask you to. Now this changes as they get older and find like-minded friends in this area, and have also adopted their own standards for purity.
- What are the boundaries you have for children playing in rooms together? It's not fear-based parenting to require doors to be open at all times, or even better, bring toys out to the living room so we can all stay together. It's not fear, it's wisdom.
- What are the boundaries you've established regarding sleep-overs? If you say yes to those special situations, you are cultivating challenges that you will likely be pressured to open up to in other situations down the road. We chose early on to say no to everyone regarding sleepovers. There's simply

nothing good that comes from it. It prevented hurt feelings or accusatory favoritism with others, and no begging from our children. For more on this topic, we have podcast episodes and teach even more in-depth on this in our Parenting Mentor Program at courageousparenting.com!

- What are the boundaries you've set for family? This is a vital marriage conversation to be had, and the most asked question when we do live Q&A's for the Parenting Mentor Program.
- What are the boundaries you set for your children regarding technology use? We believe it's vital to teach them while they are in your home, but to guide them well and at the right age. Also, how old are your children? What media have they been exposed to, and what topics need to be addressed because of the media? Gender confusing content seems to be everywhere, even in grocery stores, banks, and public libraries. Be sure you are making decisions with a realistic biblical worldview of living in a fallen world.

Children are becoming more and more promiscuous and are engaging in sexual activity at very young ages. But these children most likely were exposed to other sins like pornography first. Courageous parents must be willing to investigate if their child is struggling with any form of sexual immorality, such as pornography, fornication, or lust. We cannot assume that they are doing just fine just because we think they aren't sexually promiscuous. That is not the biblical standard. This is why it is so crucial that we teach our children about sin and what precisely not to participate in.

Remember, God cares about our hearts as much as he does our physical bodies and actions.

We are also living in a time where the number of evil people with a hunger to harm children in egregious ways is rapidly growing. At the right age, your children need to be taught about the evil in the world, the dangers, and taught to pay attention when they are away from home so that they don't fall prey to danger.

The most crucial element in teaching our children how to protect their purity comes through developing a relationship where conversations about intimacy and purity are comfortable, common, and welcome. All parents have to work at making themselves approachable on these topics. We as parents must realize that no matter how hard we try to make it comfortable for our children to talk with us, the reality is that children will feel uncomfortable talking about it most of the time. If your children have not shared about a crush before, they most likely won't ask you about intimate questions either. You need to start opening up that discussion.

Over the years, we invested in many Christian books that would help to talk about sensitive topics such as how babies are created and born, how bodies change, and what to expect, so that the topics wouldn't seem so sensitive. We began reading these books, which were age-appropriate, from the time our children were young.

Many of our children's first questions on intimate topics were prompted by mommy being pregnant. As we would read books about "How God Made Me" and read Scripture together, our children delighted in learning about the intelligent design of human anatomy. The books we read would inspire more questions, which we would answer with explanations based on their maturity. By the time our daughters were five and seven years old, they were mature enough to be at the birth of their baby brothers! Again, we embraced the events of life naturally, not awkwardly, and helped our children to get their questions answered in a way that brought God glory and prepared them for real life, and viewing birth as a natural and beautiful part of life, one that is unique and, Lord willing, would help cultivate a deeper relationship with Angie and the girls.

Sexual purity in regard to marriage is an intimate and private topic that should be taught by a parent, preferably of the same gender.

Your journey down this road may look similar to ours or different. The point is to develop approachable relationships with your children, where open communication is welcomed and comfortable. It's also essential to keep deep conversations frequent throughout life.

They never need to stop. The goal is to have developed the kind of relationship where your children feel comfortable coming to you about intimate health issues and struggles for prayer and advice as they get older and into their own parenting journey!

A Special Note on Raising Daughters from Angie:

As mothers, we also get to teach our daughters about the temptations that are common to women, such as the lust for an emotional connection with a man. We must teach them to protect their purity of heart; this includes warning them about the temptations of romance novels, romcom movies, or shows that could result in escapism and false expectations. Music also has a huge influence on humanity regarding our thoughts. God knows this and tells us in Psalm 1:1-2, "Blessed is the man who walks not in the counsel of the wicked, nor stands in the way of sinners, nor sits in the seat of scoffers; but his delight is in the law of the Lord, and on his law he meditates day and night." What we read, listen to, and meditate on impacts us greatly! This is one spiritual discipline we can teach our children to help them overcome the temptation to sin by reading the Word of God and having it written on their hearts from childhood.

I would say one of the most tempting spaces for discontentment, comparison, discouragement, jealousy, coveting, and so on is social media! Again, purity first starts in the mind with what we are focusing on, thinking about, watching, and being influenced by. Trends in clothing can also be highly influential among girls. They must be vigilant to protect their sexual purity by dressing modestly, not flirting or being promiscuous, or leading boys on, and especially by not putting themselves in dangerous situations where they can be compromised. One area I believe is needed if children are allowed to use social media is accountability with devices and communication.

Ultimately, you want your daughters to understand the biblical teaching behind modesty and have their own convictions. As your daughters get older, you shouldn't really have to have many discussions about what they wear if they have this understanding and you trust where their heart is at. Recognizing that pressure to dress certain ways is often an attempt to fit into the crowd or to find confidence through outward appearance and attention is a temptation for all girls, for crying out loud, it is a temptation for adult women! Are they trying to gain attention? Do they have low self-esteem and want people to notice them because it makes them feel better in the moment? On the other hand, if they think that super conservative dress actually makes them stand out more and they don't want to draw attention to themself at all? These are all important questions to address with your girls. If they feel pressure to dress a certain way, whether more or less conservative, because of a group of people, that is a red flag that needs to be addressed.

Lastly, I think there is a growing need for mothers to teach their daughters about the reality of the world we live in as they get older, and to teach them basic red flags to look out for in public spaces in order for them to be safe physically. Obviously, being alone, distracted by a phone, and unaware of their surroundings are all pretty typical things young girls and preteens seem to struggle with today. As parents, we need to warn our daughters for their safety and give them training in how to be alert and aware, not giving the devil a foothold.

A Special Note on Raising Sons from Isaac:

Fathers should teach their sons the importance of abstinence and protecting their sisters in Christ's hearts as well. Women can struggle with lust as much as guys; the symptoms of it may just look different. Shockingly, though, the issue of pornography among women has been growing substantially every year. It is essential to teach our sons how they are wired as well as teach them how to set boundaries to protect their eyes and ears from the temptation of sexual sin. Dads must have regular conversations with their sons about the purity of their eyes and minds, check their phones and computers for accountability, and continue the conversation.

Another necessary conversation is teaching your sons to be aware of the ways of the seductive woman, or Jezebel spirit, as the bible describes her. Throughout the Old Testament, fathers warn their sons to be wary of them and to be on the lookout for them so they can flee. Judges 16, the account of Samson and Delilah, is a prime example. Teaching our sons that God has a plan for them and that the enemy also does, and that he has used women with a Jezebel spirit to try to thwart God's purposes in the past, and what we can learn from that is so important. Even reading Proverbs 31, where King Lemuel's own mother is warning him about what kind of woman to avoid and what to look for in a wife worthy of being a Queen one day. These are all powerful passages of scripture with iconic teachings that can be a massive exhortation to young men to be aware, alert, and guard themselves. (Genesis 2:24; Prov. 5:18-20) These Scriptures are a prominent model for parents in the importance of having these tough but necessary conversations with our children.

WARNING: A rigid, threatening approach to expecting abstinence is often harshly enforced by parents who are uncomfortable discussing purity with their children. Unfortunately, these parents struggle within themselves because they are fiercely protective of the children and know the reality of the sinfulness that the culture will entice them toward. One problem with the "You will not be promiscuous" approach is that it can often sever the relationship between parent and child, leaving no one for the child to get wise advice from. Another problem with this approach is that it can rob children of the enjoyable freedom and pleasure God intends for them when they are married.

Parenting QUESTIONS

- Who is teaching your child about sex, purity, and intimate topics: you, social media, movies, friends, teachers, guidance counselors, or a youth pastor?
- One harmful lie to watch for is the belief that sex is bad. That isn't true. Sex is a beautiful gift from God when it is expressed

within the boundaries of marriage. Think of it like a fire in a fireplace: contained within the fireplace, it brings warmth and enjoyment; outside of it, the same fire can cause serious damage.

- Have you ever had "the talk" with your child regarding sex and purity? Regardless of whether others have talked to your child about sex or not, you actually need to have ongoing conversations. There may be lies that have been taught to them, which you will need to weed out and correct. One thing we teach in more depth in the Parenting Mentor program is this concept of having warm-up conversations that lead into more conversations. It's about creating comfort to come to you with questions, myths, and confusion.
- If your children are young and you have not yet discussed sexual purity, make sure you start thinking of a plan for how to engage this topic now. It's better not to be caught off guard, and you definitely don't want to be too late.
- Do you have standards set in your home regarding modesty and boundaries on technology to help protect the purity of your children?
- Are you aware that their friends and school counselors/teachers may have already begun teaching your children a non-biblical perspective on sex? Have you communicated with your child about what they have learned in school?
- Evaluate your children's peers and friends. What do they believe about sex and marriage? Are their friends like-minded? Be careful. Peers have a MASSIVE influence, especially during middle and high school years.

Courageous Parenting CHALLENGE

- Be purposeful in trying to build a relationship with your children where you are viewed as a trustworthy and wise advisor. Don't be quick to pop in answers, but get good at asking questions of your children (Proverbs 18:13). Begin the conversation about sex and purity. If possible, it is best if moms can cover this with their daughters and dads with their sons. If you haven't implemented boundaries for protecting your children's eyes from impurity and lust, make a plan and execute.

Courageous Parenting Podcasts

- Talking to Your Kids About Sex
- Protecting Your Child's Sexual Innocence
- Tough Kid Conversations and Hormones

PRAYER

Father, thank you for the gift of marriage and the pleasure that we get to experience in marriage through intimacy. Will you put a hedge of protection around our children now? We know that we must trust You above all our efforts because there will inevitably be a time when we won't have full control over their life. We desire for our children to make wise choices and not to live with sexual regret and pain. Please help us to know what to say and when. Guide us in developing a relationship with each of our children that cultivates open, honest communication about intimate issues. Protect their hearts from becoming manipulated into doing something they don't want to do. And Lord, we pray that any sins that have been committed by any parents reading this book right now would be repented of right now in the name of Jesus. Might they experience becoming clean, new, and forgiven, not allowing the enemy to have a foothold in their life that can prevent them from being fully able to teach their own children? God, we pray for any parent who is struggling with the reality that maybe their children are already deep in sexual sin. Would you give them perseverance to run the race set before them and give them the biblical counsel and wisdom in how to communicate and confront their child for the sake of their health!

Give them wisdom, Lord. In Jesus' Name, Amen.

SECTION TWO

Marriage Challenge

Begin your date night in prayer together and then look over the recap of topics covered in the second section of the book. Let the Spirit lead if there is a specific topic that needs to be addressed, be willing to talk about hard topics, and encourage one another.

Father,

Thank you for this time we have together as a married couple. We love You and want to parent our children according to Your Word and will. In many regards, we don't know what that looks like practically for each of our children. Give us wisdom, Lord, to know what we should do, what we should say, how we should say it, and what our focus with each child should be right now. Thank you for making us aware of so many opportunities we have to disciple our children and grow ourselves. Be with us tonight. May our conversation honor You, and might we grow closer to one another as well. In Jesus Name, Amen.

For reference, here are section two's chapters:

- Biblical Priorities In The Trenches
- Sowing, Reaping, & Biblical Discipline
- Humility & The Benefits of Biblical Community
- Vital Listening Skills
- How to Cultivate a Teachable Heart

- Equipped to Discern Influences Biblically
- Prepared to Navigate Friendships Biblically
- Protect, Preserve, & Equip for Purity

Discussion Questions:

- Reflect and celebrate your successes together. It's easy to be focused on where we can improve, and while that is important to growing, it is also really encouraging and empowering to acknowledge areas where you are rockin' it! Of these topics, or any that we have covered in this book so far, which are you most thankful for?
- Out of the topics covered this week, what was most convicting to you and why? Share with your spouse.
- What areas do you feel like you are doing a good job of being a team in parenting? What areas do you desire more support, help, or backup? Is there a topic where you just don't know where to begin? Talk about that as a couple, research and study the Word together, make a plan, and be in communication about it over the next few months.

Courageous Parenting CHALLENGE

- Encourage your spouse in their parenting. Think of 1-3 things that you see them doing really well and praise them for it.
- Take time sharing where you would like prayer regarding parenting and your relationships with your children. Then, after you share, pray for each other right then and there.

SECTION 03

The Skills for Thriving

CHAPTER 16

Design & Influence Your Family Culture

In the business world, team culture is deemed extraordinarily important to the success of organizations. So why is it talked about so little in regard to family?

Most people don't understand what culture really is and how to influence it in a direction. Here are some valuable answers.

Your family culture is what's true about your family. It's not the idyllic moments, your family's Sunday best, or your vision for your family. It's also not what you would say to others about your family when showing them a picture and answering their questions. For most, it's not what you would post on social media about your family, either. Additionally, it's often different from the bios about you and your family on social media profiles, too.

Again, your family culture is what's true about your family; the raw, true realities about your family. It's not your ideals for behavior; it's what the true behavior trends actually are within each person in your family, or, even better said, the behaviors of each individual when no one else is looking. This includes you.

It's also what the real norms, written or unwritten rules that people follow, are as well. It's what the real collective aspirations and sense of purpose that a family actually lives out.

Why are we defining this? Because you'll never influence a better culture until you understand what your family culture actually is. It takes real honest introspection.

See, there's always a culture within a group of people, and it's only great when leaders are purposeful and consistent at influencing it in a direction. When this isn't happening (most families), it will naturally ebb towards mediocrity, especially as children get older and other influences encroach.

Parents will see this when one parent is excited about influencing something new, the other parent gets on board, and after a while, they start to see fruit from it. But life gets busy, and they let up on this area, and they start seeing the old problems coming back again, and they become discouraged.

It's good to implement new principles; we hope you implement what you've been learning in this book. But lasting change happens when leaders (Parents) understand the good and the ugly about their current culture, then identify a few culture-driving **statements** that influence lots of the negatives to improve and commit to never stopping communicating about them. We could write a whole book on this; perhaps we will, but we at least wanted to get you started on this.

You'll never influence a better culture until you understand what your family culture actually is. It takes real honest introspection.

Here are some culture-driving statements we have purposefully made and driven in our family over many years consistently. Some of which were due to seeing changes in society that are coming as well.

- Producers versus consumers
- Eagles not seagulls
- Tolpin team

- Be generous
- Get it right at home first.

Once you identify the right culture driving statements, launch them with your family by discussing why it matters (bring meaning to it) and commit together to never stop talking about it to your children.

Most don't stay the course long enough to see the good fruit, but if you do, you will see tremendous outcomes long term.

But let's talk more in depth about Building a TEAM Culture in Your Family.

This world is harsh at times. There used to be a time when American Christians didn't think much about receiving persecution for their biblical perspectives or lifestyle choices. Today, persecution is heightening and even invading the Body of Christ in the form of division.

There is a worldly influence that has seeped into the culture of the Church today, and it has made it increasingly more difficult for believers to fully obey Christ in every area of their lives.

We all want to raise children who will "be strong in the Lord, and in the strength of his might." Eph. 6:10 We don't just want children to believe in God. We want them to know Him, have a personal relationship with the Lord, and to understand that they have a purpose for being here that is far greater than their selfish desires.

How can we raise children to be strong in the Lord, to stand firm, and stand up for righteousness in a world that is against God and His ways?

The answer to this question lies in being a member of a TEAM.

First of all, as God's holy people, chosen and dearly beloved by Him, we are a part of something larger than ourselves and more massive than our family. We are a part of the Body of Christ. So, as we attempt to raise our children in the nurturing and admonition of the Lord, we need help, wisdom, guidance, and support, which should come from the Family of God.

Do you have support?

Have you opened up your life to others in your Church in an intimate way that offers support? If not, I urge you to start.

God designed the Body of Christ, His family, with this in mind. You don't have to feel the weight of parenting alone or figuring out if what you are doing or aren't doing is biblical or beneficial.

Did you know that God cares about your character just as much as He cares about your child's? And he wants to sharpen, challenge, and grow you. One way He does this is through biblical fellowship. Believe it or not, your children need a Christian, like-minded community as well.

One day, your children are going to leave and cleave; they are going to grow up and go out.

They will need to look for and cultivate authentic, deep friendships to help them in the journey of life and all the decisions they will face. What we model for our children is paramount in helping them to have a healthy understanding of how to build a Christ-centered community. If you haven't done this yourself, they will struggle to know what it looks like, and they won't even know what they are missing.

Secondly, the family should be the first place where our children experience a TEAM culture and build safe relationships. The relational skills they learn in your home will forever impact the trajectory of their relationships in the future, either for good or bad.

You are building today the relationship you will have in the future. So be on purpose with cultivating what you desire.

From the time our children were young, we have emphasized the importance of being a team with their siblings. We would often call ourselves Team Tolpin.

We have shared with them a vision of being able to rely on one another in everything they face in life. Their relationships with one another need to be built now, with the future in mind. So they need to learn how to be a team now so that they can be a good team member when they are older.

You are building today the relationship you will have in the future. So be on purpose with cultivating what you desire.

Specifically speaking, because we live in a fallen world and have to conquer the sins of the flesh, we fail each other at times. Sin happens, and relationships are affected. But how we react to sin, hurt, selfishness, and so on is what is uncommon in our culture. We teach our children what Biblical reconciliation looks like, and we hold them accountable to it. When they are young, we walk them through how to confess, apologize, and forgive. It's one of the most critical life skills your children should be equipped with: learning how to deal with conflict and how to reconcile.

Ultimately, we express to our children that they have to get it right here, in the family, first. Other relationships outside the family are fun, and even necessary, but never at the expense of the ones that God has directly chosen for each of us: family. For your children to be supported to stand firm in Christ in modern times, they will need others willing to stand beside them. You have an opportunity to raise that support amongst all of your children!

Friends will come and go, but family will always be in your life.

Here's a HUGE WARNING: How do you expect your children to have strong sibling relationships if, as they grow up, they are increasingly separated from each other in everything they do? A family that's always going in different directions, with siblings separated into age-specific activities, is a recipe for the ruin of your hope for a strong family team.

Whether it's classrooms, sports, lessons, or even church youth ministry, it all adds up. It also sends a clear message that's only reinforced by peers that they should only be friends with people their age or a little older. The unfortunate disaster beneath the surface lies with the growing division in the hearts of your older children towards the younger.

We've been careful while raising our nine children not to do this too much. Regardless of the church we were at, all of our children sat with us during the entire church service, despite often being the only family doing so in many seasons. Our children weren't raised in youth programs at all. But they have had wonderful experiences doing their own thing at times, too. It's a balance, but we believe if you are balanced towards what yields strong family relationships, you are going to look odd to most Christians around you.

If you want strong family teamwork, stop separating your children from each other!

How do you cultivate a TEAM attitude in your family?

Pick an activity or project to cultivate teamwork amongst your children. We talked about the impact that serving together can have on a family, but there is an equal opportunity to grow relationships and team camaraderie by creating or building something together. Our family cultivated, planted, and cared for a vineyard together. Our children were young, but we weren't doing this project to make wine. We decided to cultivate a vineyard because we wanted to teach our children work ethic, as well as to have an ongoing project that we could all do together that would produce teamwork.

In the nine years that we worked on our hobby vineyard together, the most beautiful fruit that we harvested was in our hearts.

We've also done numerous long RV trips that required teamwork in close quarters, homesteading together, building the podcast shows together, and our latest project of planting a church in our hometown.

What project or vision can you share with your family to cultivate a team atmosphere?

Here are some examples:

- Work together on home projects
- Create a garden together
- Build something (a farm, a project, a business)
- Start a ministry
- Serve together (worship, missions, someone in need)

Over the last 26 years of marriage, one thing we have always done is try to make our ventures, businesses, or ministries a family pursuit where the children are able to serve and develop their skills.

When our oldest children were little, Isaac would let our son and daughter come to work with him to "help." When we would host events at our house, whether for work, ministry, or family and friends, we all worked together as a team to prepare and serve.

As you are brainstorming ideas of how you can create a team culture in your family, remember that it doesn't have to be an enormous feat; it can be as simple as weeding or washing the car together.

Parenting QUESTIONS

- ❖ What is the real culture in your family? How do people treat one another? What are the real behaviors and predominant attitudes?
- ❖ What are some influencing concepts you want to instill in your family?
- ❖ List some examples of ways your family has operated as a team, built something together, served all together, and experienced a closer bond relationally because of it. What are some new ways you could do that?

Courageous Parenting CHALLENGE

Dream with your children about events in their lives that they will undoubtedly experience, and create the vision of sharing those events with their siblings. Tell them the truth, that many friends will come and go in their lifetime, but that if they cultivate a healthy lifelong relationship with their brother/sister, they will have the unconditional and devoted support of them. You have to give vision to your children about what you dream of regarding their relationships.

Here is an example we have taught our children over the years. Imagine when you are older, and you need help with a business venture like flipping a house, or with babysitting for a date night with your spouse, who do you want to be able to call? Family is always the safest because they love you and want God's best for you!

What vision can you give your children about being a team and helping or serving one another?

Courageous Parenting PODCAST

- Creating Family Culture(Ep. 2)
- Building a New Family Culture this Summer (Ep. 194)
- Protect Your Family Culture (Ep. 282)
- Intentionally Recalibrating Family Culture (ep. 324)
- Family Culture Planning Date Night (Ep. 325)

PRAYER

Father, we know that our family is an image-bearing light to the world. And we recognize that the family is the training ground where we all learn how to work as a team so that we can be productive members of Your Body, the Family of God. We deeply desire to be a light and magnify You by the way we treat one another, and model for our children what a biblical marriage can look like, working as a team through the biblical roles You have placed us in. Please help us lead our children to work well together. Father, help us both to lead our children to truly value one another and the unique ways You created each of them, that they might not be competitive with one another. Help our children to treat one another with respect and to have a heart attitude that pleases You. May they choose to fight for family as they grow up, and be willing to repent and forgive one another, as conflict will likely be inevitable.

God, we pray for protection over our children's relationships. We acknowledge that YOU designed every family and that you chose us to be our children's parents. What an honor and privilege, Father! May we do Your will as we attempt to lead them to You and in Your way.

In Jesus' Name, Amen.

CHAPTER 17

Producers Versus Consumers

Most families allow too many escapist activities, such as reading too much fiction, watching movies or shows, excessive video gaming, or antisocial technology use. Too much of anything can be a bad thing. The natural state of things is an ever-increasing consumption. Unless parents are vigilant and purposeful, the culture of the family will be swept away into nominal versus purposeful living.

The social media age has shifted so much attention and time towards consumption of media, and now that those patterns are well established, we are now in the AI age, and unless they're proactively equipped to continue using their own creativity, those deeply ingrained consumption habits will cause them to produce even less, at least from their own minds, after all, AI will be able to produce most things. On the flip side, AI can be incredibly helpful for those who have developed the right convictions in how to utilize it with appropriate boundaries. In fact, your children can become more productive in pursuing their dreams at even a younger age!

It's not that our children don't consume media; they do. Producers versus consumers was launched in 2018 at a new year planning meeting with our family as one of our family's culture driving statements that has stayed with us ever since. "Producers versus Consumers" is short for: make sure you produce more than you consume. In other words, don't just watch people living their dreams; work the muscle of producing and living your dreams.

We saw the direction everything was going and established a strong statement to influence discipline in our children to use their minds in ways that contribute to society in alignment with who God made them to be.

What's interesting about AI is that those who have a producer mentality can now actually produce more than ever before, but those who have a consumption mentality will probably consume more than ever before while losing belief in the gifts God gave them.

Just like social media makes the depressed more depressed, AI will make the lazy more lazy. The disciplined (Producers) will be even more productive using AI tools to scale their creations. But here's a huge warning: make sure you create discipline with your children to not let AI steal their minds or their creativity. What we mean is, when it comes to creating their original art, make sure they still do that, whether it's writing, lyrics, or paintings.

It's going to take tremendous discipline that must be ingrained in their minds while they are in their home, so they don't just let AI do it all for them.

This is one of those areas in parenting, where it is hard to lead by example, and let's just be honest, IT'S EXHAUSTING to be diligent.

If we are to equip our children by helping them to build healthy habits, it's going to cost us something. Raising producers versus consumers will cost you in time, money, and sleep.

This challenge is not for the faint of heart.

Since we are preparing children for greater unprecedented times, they need to know how to create what others will consume and experience all that comes with that. Most importantly, our children will learn how to experience rejection. Another signature aspect of producing something is the satisfaction that comes in witnessing someone else enjoy what you have created.

For example, our daughters love to cook, specifically bake. I witnessed this being instilled and encouraged in them when they were younger as they helped Angie in the kitchen and loved watching me, Dad, enjoy the tasty treats they worked so hard to create.

Was there a sacrifice in cultivating a desire to cook and bake well in my daughters? If you asked Angie, she would say yes, but it was worth it. It was a messy job, but she knew it would be a way to connect with the girls long term, and she wanted them both to be comfortable in the kitchen, prepared and equipped for homemaking when they were older.

She recognized that choosing the easier, more convenient approach to parenting can lead to raising children who are bored, idle, and mentally unprepared for the challenges of a rapidly changing world. It's increasingly risky to rely solely on traditional employment. They need to have experience producing, as this will help set them apart and guide them as they forge their paths. The ability to dream, envision, and create will open doors to new freedoms that can give opportunities to your child for truly leaving a lasting legacy.

The world doesn't respond to knowledge alone; it responds to results and experience. Consuming knowledge is important, but what will prepare your children for a different world is experience, putting that knowledge into practice. Adding their knowledge to their God-given creativity and producing something others will use or consume is mandatory in preparing our children for the next generation. If we are raising children to lead in the next generation, we must rise above the norm of consumer obsession and addiction.

You've got to go beyond the lemonade stand, too!

You've never heard a successful leader stand on stage, look back with fond memories of their lemonade stand, and entitle it as the signature moment in their childhood that got them desiring to do something transformational.

If we are going to raise courageous Christian children who are going to become influential in taking back every industry for the glory of God, we have to protect our children from the addiction of idleness and free them to become the best version of themselves. The parents who rise to this challenge are courageous by being willing to set boundaries, engage their children, allow them opportunities to produce and be inventive, but they also have the ability to dream with their children.

Yes, we want our children to be familiar with how to use technology, but not at the expense of numbing creativity out of every spark of genius God put in their minds. Internet, Technology, AI, and social media should be engaged on purpose; for a purpose, with a purpose, and limited to a specific goal which has an end. We need to cultivate in our children a spiritual discipline of balance in all areas of our lives. To be able to give all of ourselves to a task at hand, work hard, think smart, and finish what we start, but we also need to teach them how to just be and think. Being a producer takes brain energy and requires rejuvenation. It requires believing in themselves and in how God made them. Authenticity, refreshing, and growth in confidence don't happen by consuming entertainment or other people's lives.

When we talk to our children about the difference between being a producer or a consumer, it is best explained as creating vs. being entertained by what is created. We shouldn't always need to be entertained by something flashing at us. Instead, we need to train our children in the fine arts of being quiet, thinking, journaling, dreaming, envisioning, building, and discussing. These were commonplace before entertainment technology.

Additionally, they will need to become trained in the effective use of some of the AI tools and future technologies as things progress, as discussed in a coming chapter.

Families would regularly discuss politics, relationships, faith, work, ideas, philosophy, and enjoy reading classical literature together. These characteristics of strong families found in the 1800-1900's are slowly being eroded. Now, you are lucky to find families eating dinner together and discussing their days, what they are learning, world events, and praying together.

Mediocrity is constantly pushing on the family, specifically through easy-to-consume, readily available media. The parents who cultivate a "producer" culture within their families are constantly influencing against this wind of mediocrity. They recognize the battle, set boundaries, educate their children on what technology is meant to be used for (a tool), and they encourage deep thinking and conversations.

Parenting QUESTIONS

- ❖ Would you define your children's habits as being producers or consumers?
- ❖ How much time per day do your children spend consuming?
- ❖ What changes do you observe in your children after they have been using technology?
- ❖ How could family relationships be changed or different if device usage were appropriate?
- ❖ What boundaries do you believe need to be in place to create radical change in your family?
- ❖ What changes do you observe in your children after they have been using technology?
- ❖ How could family relationships be changed or different if device usage were appropriate?
- ❖ What boundaries do you believe need to be in place to create radical change in your family?

Entrepreneurial Ideas (Producing)

- Making jewelry
- Blog
- Virtual assistant business
- Make crafts
- Sewing products to be sold in local shops
- Seamstress (Hemming, Alterations)
- Bakery: Sourdough, Bread, Scones, Desserts
- Food Truck
- Write a book, a poem, or a song
- Landscaping, painting, or window cleaning business venture
- Create an app or video game

- Teach piano or music lessons
- Detailing Business (cars)
- Photography
- Baking goods
- Playing Music at a Nursing Home
- Record Music
- Video blogs
- Build courses
- Create a service business
- House cleaning business
- Build handcrafted, useful wooden furniture or art
- Build a technology company

Courageous Parenting CHALLENGE

- ❖ Help your children evaluate if they are spending too much time watching other people live their dreams, or if they are spending enough time working on their own dreams.
- ❖ Tonight's challenge is to think about how you could lessen consumption and increase production in your home. Discuss it with your spouse and try to implement this practical change in your day-to-day family life.

Courageous Parenting PODCAST

- Pursue Family Projects that Require Team Work Part 1 (Ep.122)
- Pursue Family Projects that Require Team Work Part 2 (Ep.123)

PRAYER

Father, we want to glorify You and fulfill one of our purposes to cultivate and create good, useful, and helpful goods. Help us to raise our children in a way that is productive. Give us inspiration, ideas, and wisdom as we guide our children. We know that You warn us against the sin of idleness, of becoming a sluggard. Help us to be vigilant in our parenting, that we might raise children to live on purpose for You.

In Jesus Name, Amen.

CHAPTER 18

Social Media, Gaming, & Internet Access

There was a day when people thought social media was a trend and wouldn't last. Now, social media has become an integrated aspect of social life and is intertwined in most young people's lives. As a parent, you have the responsibility and privilege to teach and model social interaction to prepare your children to engage this social world intentionally and in a way that brings glory to God.

The truth is that you can likely protect your child from experiencing a lot of the foolish pains that many youth are experiencing today as a result of being on social media if you choose to create a boundary that is a hard no regarding social media until they are older teenagers The testimonies and stats on children experiencing cyber-bullying, fomo (fear of missing out), comparison trap, jealousy, coveting, depression, and even in some cases victims of dangerous predators is staggering. Some parents would argue that they are operating in reality and protecting their children, which would be wise, to a certain degree. The reality that we also must face is that social media is a part of our world now, and that in the distant future, children will eventually be young adults and likely need to be familiar with navigating media either for work or to decide to be there for relational reasons.

With that reality in mind, we believe there is a happy medium balance that is appropriate in most circumstances. Of course, in some cases, serious protection might be required indefinitely. But in most cases, we would recommend delayed involvement entirely until there is a spiritual and emotional maturity that is attained. Once they are mature enough, there should be a duration of time where there is, monitoring for accountability, teaching, and ideally this would be closer to the time when the teen is closer to launching into the real world. It is important that your children learn healthy uses and boundaries of these platforms while in the environment of your home, with accountability and safety. The testimonies of parents of adult children who have become victims of the influences of social media are enough to convince us that it is crucial that you lead your children in a biblical worldview of these platforms.

At what age do I let my child use social media?

First of all, this is not an age-specific answer, but rather a spiritual maturity issue, although most social engines do have age limitations and restrictions. What we mean by spiritual maturity is that not all of your children are going to model the same maturity or understanding at the same age. Not only that, but some may choose that it's best for them not to even engage on social media at all.

Here is a good test: Does your child exhibit self-control in other areas of his/her life? If they do, they may be ready for fewer limitations regarding social media than another child. If they do not, they either might not be prepared for social media at all, or you will have to be more hands-on in monitoring and guiding. That is up to you.

One thing is for sure, though: If your child is on social media, you need to be. If you are scared of it because you don't know how to use it, then be honest with yourself and engage in the learning process. You will be modeling for them that you can enjoy learning new things, but also that you care about what matters to them.

Are you aware of everything your child is doing on social media?

If you haven't invested time in getting educated on the different social media platforms your children are using, stop what you are doing right now and begin that journey. You need to be aware that there are social engines that allow children to post videos and images that will be deleted within a few hours of being published, making accountability to the user difficult. This lack of monitoring and accountability is why you must be vigilant to be on the lookout for bullying, sexting (sex texting), and intimate relationships forming, including predators pursuing your teen.

Video games and numerous chat apps are also used by predators to groom children. It doesn't matter to list them out; what matters is that you are vigilant to know what your children are doing on anything that's digital, but that's impossible if they don't have a teachable heart towards you. It's also impossible if you haven't cultivated a relationship where they are comfortable talking to you about personal and tough things.

It's vital that you have an open relationship where you can discuss these kinds of topics with your children because these are the kinds of tools the devil would love to use to snag your sweet child to tempt them to sin, hurt your relationship with them, steal them away, or even plant seeds of doubt in God.

You have the authority to set boundaries for your children. Internet services and technology used in your family are your jurisdiction and responsibility. Lead your children in righteousness regarding how to engage in social media. If your children rebel against the boundaries you set, they need to experience healthy, biblical consequences. You are the parent. Consequences are God's design for teaching us all; that we reap what we sow, and a parent must utilize this life reality appropriately to "train a child in the way he should go."

Teach your children about the dangers of social media, video games, and chat rooms. Help them understand the repercussions and temptation for sin, but also the power that they can use these tools to influence others as well. Be purposeful and excited for them to begin having more impact!

When you see your child using social media purposefully, praise them.

When you see things you don't like or approve of, don't be harsh in your approach. Pray first, take a deep breath, and ask open-ended questions to get to the bottom of the issue. Realize that what you are seeing is a reflection of your leadership, or lack thereof. Take responsibility and apologize. Don't assume that if your child looks like the golden child in the real world, they are golden in the digital world.

It is crucial that, as a parent, you are not a hypocrite regarding engagement with social media. Remember that your children are watching you. Do you and your husband hold one another accountable? If not, you should. When you got married, God united you, and He designed you to be a team. How you engage social media can be a HUGE blessing to others and a light to the lost.

Don't assume that if your child looks like the golden child in the real world, they are golden in the digital world.

INTERNET SAFETY:

Imagine yourself as a child. Left to your imagination, where would Google lead you? Where would AI lead you?

Our children are growing up in an age of easy access to everything. They are searching for whatever they want to know, watching videos on it, and learning from someone you have not approved of.

You are a negligent parent if you haven't established a relationship with your child to filter their online activity. Every human needs accountability on this. If you are not holding your child accountable, you are leaving your child vulnerable to all kinds of information, both good and bad.

Remember that technology, social media, AI, phones, and other electronic devices are not inherently good or bad. These are neutral, amoral tools, which can be used for both compelling, redemptive reasons as well as harmful, deceiving purposes; however, the reality is that the people controlling AI, media, and social media platforms will be operating out of their worldview and convictions. In fact, it's proven that most platforms have a left-leaning bias that easily influences the populace in unholy thinking.

Never let your child buy their phones, because you want to have control of them. At what age do they get a phone? What are the rules around having a phone? Again, we believe this will vary from family to family and child to child, depending on maturity and trust. You can educate your child, empower them by trusting them, and establish solid and clear boundaries, then go for it. But don't drop the ball; stay diligent with checking their phones and search history.

If you are not careful, games and laughter in your home will disappear. The house will become silent with the glow of a screen upon every child's face. Family connections and conversations will become burdensome and unenjoyable as the impatience from expecting everything to be communicated quickly on their time will literally change all human interactions. Help your child develop good habits for using technology. It is a tool, not a toy.

We recommend evaluating your standards for what you allow your children and yourselves to see through technology and create clear expectations.

God's word urges us to be vigilant in protecting our hearts by protecting our eyes and ears. It's one way we can proactively pursue purity. He gave us spiritual armor because we have a ruthless enemy who seeks to destroy us and our relationships. He wants to make us ineffective for the Kingdom. We have to be alert for attacks that could come through technology or social media. "Behold, I am sending you out as sheep in the midst of wolves, so be wise as serpents and innocent as doves." Matthew 10:16, ESV

Here are some suggestions for boundaries you might want to discuss with your spouse and implement with your children:

- Limit screen time per day (EMF waves) and check it using an app.
- Limit weekly screentime, including all technology, movies, social media, and video games. Also, make sure you are aware of how much time each week and per day your child spends on the computer or technology for school and pleasure.

- Have your children read a book for an hour before being able to do any screentime.
- Set the standard that all homework and chores need to be completed before even asking for screentime.
- Never allow devices in bathrooms.
- Do not allow devices in bedrooms without the accountability of another person.
- Make sure you have access to every device and randomly do weekly checks on all history and messaging on social media.
- Monitor and moderate your child's followers, friends, messaging, and connections on social media.
- Teach your children social media etiquette, check and teach them to edit their grammar.
- Give your children a vision and teach them the WHY behind even being on social media. Teach them that social media is one part of our world and that it is an opportunity to be a missionary. You must also teach your children how to evaluate if they can handle social media or if they are tempted to compare, become discontent, or are experiencing escapism.
- One other concept we teach our children regarding technology is to evaluate if they are leaning more towards being consumers or producers. We want to evaluate which category our time on technology most closely aligns with.

Parenting QUESTIONS

- ❖ Do you model for your children being a light for Christ on social media?
- ❖ Do you spend your time on social media wisely? Are you purposeful when you are on social media, or do you waste time scrolling and then spend time gossiping about what you see or read?
- ❖ Does your social media engagement take the place of your time with God? Are you in your Bible as much as you are

looking at your mobile device? What are you modeling for your children?

- ❖ Have you developed the type of relationship with your child where they can come to you for advice? Are your children willing to share what they are seeing and who they're connecting with through social media, text messaging, and email?

Courageous Parenting CHALLENGE

- ❖ Search your children's social media networks.
- ❖ Who are they following, and whose posts are they commenting on?
- ❖ Who is following them and commenting on their pictures?
- ❖ Who are their friends?

If your child isn't on social media yet, spend time learning about the different social media engines, and make decisions in alignment with your spouse about which ones you will allow and at what age.

If your older children are on social media, when they are first getting started, it's important to encourage them and teach them how to navigate it safely and with a mission. This can be everything from formatting their posts, the content, with an intent to be a light, to having you help them navigate dealing with messaging from strangers. One other recommendation is to have their account set to private with strict parental limitations.

Remember that the social media engines that your children' s friends might like the most are probably the ones that most parents are least familiar with.

Talk with your spouse about what boundaries you want to set as a family. Develop a family plan of engagement concerning social media and technology.

We recommend having a one-on-one or one-on-two meeting with your more mature teen to go over some basic rules of etiquette, expectations, limitations, and to equip them on how to handle certain potential threats or influences they may encounter.

Here are four missional and vision questions we recommend going over in your meeting with your older teenager:

1. What is your purpose or goal for being on social media?
2. What are the objectives you feel will help you to accomplish your mission and purpose?
3. How do you want to use social media to help you fulfill your purpose or goal?
4. What boundaries do you feel you need to put in place in order for you to use social media in a self-controlled and disciplined manner?

God has called all of us to be lights in this world, but also to go and make disciples of ALL NATIONS! That is exciting! How can you use social media for God's glory and the advancement of His Kingdom?

Then write a special commitment or prayer to the Lord …

Courageous Parenting PODACST

- How to Raise Kids in a Social Media World (Ep. 20)
- True Dangers of Screen Time for Kids (Ep. 302)

PRAYER

Father God, we realize that You have instructed us, as our children's parents, to teach them what is appropriate and what is not regarding how to engage on social media. Help us to model for our children what it looks like to be on purpose for Your glory. Give us wisdom as to what boundaries my child needs regarding the social media world and other technology. It is easy for us to become afraid of losing control, and that entices us to be controlling rather than taking the time to learn something new and then teach it. Give us courage and help us not to make decisions based upon fear. We know you have not given us a spirit of fear, but of power and love, and a sound mind. Help us make biblical discernments in creating boundaries regarding technology and our children. Guide us every step as a parent and help us to trust you.

In Your Son's name, Amen.

CHAPTER 19

Christian Parenting In An AI World

You can't write a parenting book about equipping your children for unprecedented times unless there's direction on making sure your children are both getting equipped to be effective with AI tools before they launch from your home, but you've also instilled the right boundaries to have while utilizing this technology.

Are there huge potential future threats to humanity because of AI? We believe there absolutely are, but this is where your parenting comes in to instill in them the important guardrails.

AI is an unavoidable change that presents parents with a double-edged sword. On the one hand, intentional Christian parents likely have thoughts of disdain for where AI is likely to take society, which would be sound thinking, actually.

Here are some negative possibilities that AI could likely usher in:

- Elimination of a large number of jobs.
- Harm to brain development and creative skills by over-relying on AI to create for them.
- Plagiarism.
- Difficulty in knowing what direction to prepare your children for.
- Greater economic disparity amongst the population.

- Nefarious agenda towards conforming the populace in evil directions.
- AI turning on humans someday.

When you read those, it almost makes you want to opt out of AI altogether and skip the rest of the chapter, BUT DON'T!

Here's an important example that will help you think about where society is going and why it's actually vital your children know how to use the right AI tools (at the age you discern is wise).

The story of two plumbing companies:

Why did we choose plumbing? Because it's one of the industries that is the most AI-resistant. Meaning AI won't be able to do plumbing anytime soon.

Let's say both companies have the same metrics as each other, with 10 employees, the same revenue, the same expenses, and both have great leaders.

We will call them plumbing companies A and B.

Plumbing company A deeply cares for its employees and dismisses AI as irrelevant for its business; after all, it doesn't understand technology and continues forward as it always has been, doing great work, providing jobs for its productive team, and delivering for customers.

Plumbing company B has all the same sentiments and characteristics except for one difference. He sees what the owner of company A doesn't see regarding AI. He realizes that his business will become less competitive as more businesses leverage AI tools and that it's essential for his company to excel by using them.

He starts to realize that there are a lot of small administrative things and route planning that plumbers do that AI systems could support them with, causing greater efficiencies, enabling each plumber to help more customers each week. Additionally, he realizes his wonderful receptionist isn't needed anymore; AI can seamlessly do what she does, and while he wants to provide a job for her, it's an expense he can't justify anymore since others in the market are becoming more efficient using AI in the same ways.

Additionally, the owner of company B can now use AI to better organize jobs, make sure inventory/supplies are ordered, and make sure trucks are always operationally ready, as well as other administrative tasks he used to do. He also realizes that he can use AI to market his business at the same capacity as a marketing agency for a fraction of the cost.

Plumbing company B now has an owner who no longer has busy work and can work on his business more easily, saving more time. Each of his employees has more customers to meet with and can accomplish more each day. And as much as they enjoyed the receptionist, there were fewer costly errors and more efficiencies happening without her.

The owner can now keep his business operating and even afford to lower his prices if needed, making him more competitive in the industry, or if he wants, he can scale it up so much more easily.

Plumbing company A is faced with a hard reality. He doesn't understand why it's getting harder and harder to get customers and feels tremendous pressure to lower his prices as his competitors become more efficient than he is. He's forced to let go of plumbers one by one over time, and pretty soon, he's down to three, but revenue isn't strong enough to pay for a receptionist. After all, he can handle that himself now that the business is smaller. Pretty soon, he remembers easier days just being a plumber without the responsibility and pressure of so much overhead. So he lets go of his last employees, gets rid of his office space, and he's now working as a sole plumber. But he's working hard day in and out, which is great, but he's becoming increasingly disillusioned since he's not charging as much as he used to in the good old days, and starts wondering what will be of his future.

This is a simple example of one of the industries that will be the most resilient as AI advances, and yet, how essential it is that the business owner is experienced in implementing the best AI tools currently available.

Not everyone is going to be a business owner, so let's look at an employee example.

Let's say two young adults who have the same talent and ability work in the same company and with the same job.

Let's say they are both salespeople in their early twenties.

Salesperson A and salesperson B.

Salesperson A is exceeding benchmarks and is seen as a valuable contribution to the company.

Salesperson B is seen in the same way at first; however, he starts to see how he can use AI Agents, which are AI tools directed to work on his behalf behind the scenes in an automated way to amplify his in-person efforts, such as automating his follow-up, improving prospect tracking, and keeping more leads warm. Perhaps even closing some sales without him, but directing him when he's needed in person. Soon, he's surpassing what's ever been done before because he's been able to utilize AI tools to make him as effective as a team of people who are in perfect sync with his daily efforts, but it's just him working the same hours. The difference is the team of AI agents working for him for almost free, enabling him to only do his most important result-creating work.

All of a sudden, he's the one getting the bonuses and the respect of not only his sales manager but the executives as well. He quickly becomes far more valuable than a salesperson in their eyes, as those same principles he's using in sales could be utilized throughout the company.

Meanwhile, salesperson A becomes prideful and has resentment because he thought he was a better salesperson than salesperson B, yet he can no longer hit the new benchmarks that have been set by salesperson B. Even if that were true, that he has more talent, he has no chance without the AI agents supporting his efforts like B does.

Salesperson B moves up to sales manager, but additionally keeps getting asked by the VPs of different departments how they can implement AI to amplify their efforts as well. The sales team starts soaring, and unfortunately, he has to let salesperson A go since he was resistant to change, causing him to achieve outdated results.

New Sales Manager B keeps advancing since he's a lynchpin in the company now and is causing huge efficiency growth, driving down expenses while increasing revenues at the same time. After work, he shares with his new wife how unfortunate it is that his help with the company has caused numerous people to lose their jobs, and she encourages him that without his help, he wouldn't have a job either, as the company would have lost its competitiveness and would have been in danger since its competitors have been scaling up AI integrations as well.

The conversation lands on the fact that these are unprecedented times that are full of opportunity, but only for those who are resilient, always learning, and willing to change.

So, do you think your older children should learn how to utilize AI before they leave your home? We believe it's a resounding yes. It's not an option, actually. You love them, you want them to thrive and be able to make progress in life.

Here's another example you can use with your children: Henry Ford created the assembly line for vehicle manufacturing. What would have happened if the other car manufacturers refused to adopt this methodology because they felt that it would lose the art of car-making? If they kept their way, they would have no company at all anymore.

Now we believe that without well-defined guardrails instilled while your children are in your home, the utilization of AI could be harmful. Now remember, fear is the worst motivator; it often causes parents to make decisions that they think are in wisdom but they are corrupted by their fear, causing long-term harm or limitations to their children.

Fear-based parenting decisions usually backfire at some point.

While we don't fully understand all of the repercussions that could exist in the future of AI, here are what we believe to be useful disciplines with AI to instill.

Isaac had a meeting with our older children, still in the home, ages 10 - 19, about the importance of learning how to utilize AI without losing their art.

Art being anything in their direction of giftedness that they would normally create on their own, they shouldn't use AI for that purpose. For example, if marketing isn't their gift, it probably makes sense to let AI help them come up with marketing copy, or titles that will be attractive to others on YouTube, and so forth.

However, they should never let AI replace their God-given voice for them, written or otherwise, or create their drawing or artwork either. Don't leave it there, though. People rarely adopt things unless they fully understand why it's important.

Let us give you a full picture of how your children can be differentiated in an increasingly homogeneous future. **They are well-versed in utilizing AI tools and platforms to help them do their original art better.**

Unfortunately, this isn't what most are going to do; in fact, most will likely fall into two unfortunate categories:

- AI users automating and replacing their own voice and art
- Hard workers without using AI

The repercussions are large in both of these common directions, the second one of which we already covered in the example above, but let's take a look at number one.

Make sure your children are well-versed in utilizing AI tools and platforms to help them do their original art better.

We believe that if people, especially young people, start letting AI produce their creativity for them, it will increasingly cause their gifts to be diminished. Humans tend to make choices in the direction of least resistance. You have to instill courage in your children to choose harder paths.

The moment they have AI write their paper, write their blog post, write their script for their video content, create their art that in the past they would have put their name on, and it returns something back that they are impressed with, their confidence in producing their own art will be diminished.

Additionally, in a matter of moments, AI produces what may have taken them hours before. It becomes an addictive drug they can't shake. The rationalization sets in: "This makes me get everything done so much faster, so I can focus on what I want."

The journey is where the growth is right? Not anymore for most. The creative journey in this regard disappears for most as it's replaced with giving prompts to technology with instantaneous results.

Instill in your children their ability to create in their directions of giftedness, be an example to them in your own life, in how you use technology.

But if they are disciplined (just like with anything), there's a new positive impact of leveraging the right technologies to accomplish things.

You are wondering how it's positive that most of the jobs today will be gone in the future? Well, it's not positive for everyone, but make sure it's positive for your family and legacy. That's our job, to equip our children, but the difference today is that you have to equip for a drastically different future than you yourself have experienced.

So be encouraged, there's tremendously good news for you and your family if you take the right actions.

The barriers to entry have disappeared for your children to create, produce, and run things, including a business.

1. Your child can now create technology solutions without ever learning a line of code.
2. The technology you build doesn't require investment.
3. Your child can now build and run things without having to build a team of employees.

4. Your child can now make whatever job they do streamlined so as to focus on the most important work itself and excel faster.
5. It's now easier for your child to differentiate themselves.
6. Your child can now use their original art (Giftedness) and leverage technology to bring it to life faster, cheaper, and in a scalable way without risk.

But here's the big one: in a world with shorter attention spans, children can make progress so much faster than ever before, **causing them to flourish and grow in confidence.** At a younger age, they can get a taste of a larger contribution to society more quickly.

They can literally think of an idea and start building it, with little to no financial risk. This stimulates minds in really powerful ways. There is a creativity involved in thinking through how to guide technology to create, which spurs a different kind of confidence as limits to their creativity disappear.

It can be highly empowering and energize your young person.

The tools themselves are always changing, so we won't recommend any here, but this is a chapter both parents must read to foster a productive discussion and to research the best paths to get up to speed.

Sometimes, a lack of knowledge and experience in something you realize is important can cause discouragement or even anxiety. While that's not the purpose of sharing this with you, if you do feel that way, prayer and action are the best solutions.

If you homeschool or not, this must become part of the training you give to your children one way or another. Also, don't think you have to know about this to help your children learn this.

Learn it and do it together.

That's what we did and are doing in the Tolpin home!

Parenting QUESTIONS

- ❖ Have you taught your children or talked about ethical, moral, or biblical boundaries regarding the usage of AI?

- ❖ What is your first step towards experiencing the practical benefits of using AI tools yourself?

Courageous Parenting CHALLENGE

- ❖ Have your spouse read this and discuss it together.
- ❖ Do research on a starting place, possibly even taking a course on it.
- ❖ Establish your guardrails to teach your children.
- ❖ Learn with your children.

Courageous Parenting PODCAST

- Christian Perspectives on AI (Ep. 240)
- Raise Your Kids to Love What's Real in an AI World (Ep. 343)
- Don't Let AI Steal Your Child's Mind(Ep. 392)

PRAYER

Father, thank you for your love and wisdom and for purposefully choosing us to parent our children. Guide us in equipping them for a different future ahead. Would you convict our hearts on what the important guardrails are to teach our children on AI? Would you help our marriage be unified as we take steps in equipping our children in the new ways of utilizing technology? Help us know how to preserve and encourage the giftedness in our children while helping them be effective in the future. We pray that our children would be convicted by their faith in you to uphold ethical and biblical standards for themselves regarding the usage of AI in the future. God, we pray for our children to be people of strong integrity and character, and that they would value human contribution through their love for others and You. May you be glorified through our legacy.

Amen

CHAPTER 20

Work Ethic & Integrity Vs. Entitlement

"The best and wisest thing in the world is to work as if it all depended upon you, and then trust in God, knowing that it all depends upon him."

-Charles Spurgeon

The Bible has much to say about work. In Genesis, God reveals to us that ONE reason He created us, aside from relationships with Him and others, is to care for the earth--to till the land and care for the creation. In the New Testament, God emphasizes our uniqueness in Christ. He has dispersed gifts and talents among the Body that are to help us fulfill God's plan for all humankind, as well as the individual enjoyment and purpose for which He knit us together in our mother's womb. But today, the generations are plagued with a heart attitude that mocks the idea of taking pleasure in working. And this sinful heart attitude of entitlement and laziness is contagiously spreading like gangrene in the West.

The Bible warns against not working and providing for one's family, saying, "But if anyone does not provide for his relatives, and especially for members of his household, he has denied the faith and is worse than an unbeliever." 1 Timothy 5:8, ESV

The parable of the talents reveals to us that we must steward the gifts, skills, and abilities we have to make a profit for the Glory of our Master, who is Christ Jesus! (Matthew 25:14-30)

Heart attitudes are cultivated, shaped, and molded through example, teaching, and accountability. We cannot expect our children to delight in working if we don't. We cannot speak with them about working for the glory of the Lord if we don't. We have another incredible opportunity to model for our children what hard work looks like, and also what it looks like to surrender to the Lord. Our character is refined as we grow a heart that enjoys working. When we wake up on purpose, thrilled to impact the world, delighted in our work, and even excited to take care of our bodies so that we can serve Him longer, we are leaving a legacy of work ethic and vision.

Work Ethic is not something that you learn or teach in one day; it is something that you work out in your soul through rigorous, steadfast daily work habits. If you want to teach your children to have a work ethic, you must be prepared that this is not something that will be a weekend-long lesson. No, this is a lifelong lesson that will require your dedication, loyalty, and leadership.

The future of work has more uncertainties than ever before, but there's always an opportunity. While work ethic is vital, as you learned from the previous chapter, so is working smarter. While working smarter has always been helpful, it will become required to thrive. It used to be that you could just work hard in a direction and succeed; that's less true in the future. The future belongs to those who have a strong work ethic and leverage technology to work smarter, too.

But leveraging technology is a moot point if there's no work ethic in the first place.

> ***The future belongs to those who have a strong work ethic and leverage technology to work smarter, too.***

However, if they only have a work ethic, it will likely mean they will be in a mode of working for someone fighting for fewer jobs in a world where there's more motivation for all to work hard when there's likely greater scarcity for jobs.

Employers will be looking for a new kind of resiliency that incorporates both work ethic and working smarter by leveraging the right technology. So it's a good idea that your children experience doing both while they are in your home.

Help your children develop a mindset of constant and never-ending improvement as they work. In the beginning, you will teach them some aspect of the work they are doing around the house, or on the property, or when serving others. But after they get going, encourage them to think about how it can be done even better. What technology could we use to streamline things and make us more effective? Or perhaps it's a discussion that leads to looking into how to leverage technology to make it streamlined.

This won't be essential for completing your home projects, shopping, chores, or serving others, but it helps them exercise the muscle that needs strengthening for combining working hard and smarter, which is essential for thriving in their future.

Your children having a strong work ethic is vital in the moment of decision on whether to take an average path that's easier, or a better path that's harder. If they value hard work and have strong character, they will choose the harder paths that are more fruitful in life.

A strong work ethic coincides with better decision-making, which becomes paramount in a future that will further reinforce the path of comfort and ease.

Just as cultivating a team atmosphere can incorporate instilling a work ethic in your child, teaching a work ethic can also develop a team atmosphere. This will come more naturally to some children. Stay diligent in teaching work ethic. It will reap a reward in their hearts, but it will also impact your grandchildren and their children.

If you want your children to become influential, productive citizens who are giving their highest and best contribution to the world for the glory of God, it begins with a good work ethic as they are entering the workforce or starting a business.

Exercise: What project can you delegate to your child that will be long-term and teach them a work ethic, as well as allow them to reap the monetary benefits?

QUESTIONS FOR DADS

- What are your first steps to teaching your children to work harder and smarter?
- Are you modeling for your children what it looks like to enjoy working?
- Do your children see you producing or consuming?
- Do you take care of your vehicle to work on your body?
- Think about how you can involve your child in your work.
- Can you take your child to work with you once a week, a month?
- Think of an opportunity where you can teach your child how to work by showing them what you do.

QUESTIONS FOR MOMS

- Do you enjoy your work? Do you find the greater purpose in even the most mundane duties and responsibilities? What about your work around the home? Or do you struggle with grumbling and complaining?
- Do your children see you have a bad attitude while you are serving your husband, cooking dinner, doing laundry, and homeschooling? Evaluate yourself in all your jurisdictions on a scale of 1-5, one being a lousy attitude, five being the best example ever.
- What can you do to encourage your children to create?
- What are some alternative activities you can invest in that will encourage delight-directed study and creativity?

Courageous Parenting CHALLENGE

- Talk to your children about how God made us all to work and to glorify Him in it. Help them to see the bigger opportunity to shine a light for Jesus in our workplaces by how we treat others and the example we are when we work hard with a good attitude.
- Try to find an opportunity to affirm your children in having good attitudes about working. One thing we have tried to teach our children is to have a "happy heart" because God cares most about our heart attitudes.

Courageous Parenting PODCAST

- Instilling Work Ethic in an Entitled World (Ep. 50)
- Chores, Teamwork, and Why We Don't Give Allowances (Ep. 51)
- Raising Thankful Kids: Defeating Whining, Complaining, and Grumbling (Ep. 262)

PRAYER

Father, we know that one of our purposes on earth is to work, and we know that you call us to delight in working, whatever that work is that You give us. Help us to have an honoring attitude towards the work You have given us to do. Help us to be thankful for it. As we attempt to teach our children and instill a work ethic in their character, would You speak to their hearts? Help them to take pleasure in working and being compensated. We pray for opportunities for our children to work hard and be paid a good wage for their work. We pray they experience the pleasure that comes from working hard and earning a good reward.

In Jesus' Name, Amen.

CHAPTER 21

Social Awareness & Communication Skills

Regardless of your education choice, as a parent, you will need to be proactive in teaching your child communication skills and how to be socially aware. Emotional intelligence is massively lacking today. It's the ability to recognize others' and one's own emotions and deal with them in an understanding and kind way, while being able to be observant of the social cues given by others as well. Being socially aware goes beyond social graces or etiquette and actually incorporates social graces while also being able to discern what the people in the room need from you and how they are responding to others. Some are better than others at this naturally, but we want to encourage you that this can be taught. Most parents just brush off bad behaviors like interrupting and use the excuse that it's just children, but the thing is, yes, they may be children, but children can learn, and it would be in your best interest and theirs if they learn that interrupting is rude, earlier rather than later.

Technological advances have progressed in many industries and professions. However, because of how accessible and addictive entertainment and social media have become for children, they are growing more antisocial than ever before. The fact that they can simply sit silent, rather than face-to-face with actual humans, and comment on some pithy remark and have zero relational consequences for it, is a sign of how the way of the world has negatively influenced the most basic communicative skills called disagreeing respectfully. Another downfall of this technological era is that the immediacy of response that we have all grown accustomed to has cultivated a selfish appetite in communication, an expectancy of immediate gratification. While we are grateful for many technological advances, the reality is that children are less trained than ever before in how to have respectful, engaging conversations.

For years, one of the biggest hurdles that people foresaw for homeschooled children was socialization. Will children be socially awkward if they are homeschooled? If socialization teaches a child how to communicate, then why in the world would I put them in one room with thirty children all the same age? That is NOT going to prepare them for real life. Segregation of generations is not God's design, but rather man's idea. He not only wants us to know how to communicate with those in the same season of life as us, but also those of all ages and stages. It is evident in Titus chapter two that His design is for us to learn from those older than us. How will our children be challenged to grow in maturity? What social graces will my child learn by being segregated from other age groups of children?

Courageous parents must proactively teach their children to have the confidence to look an adult in the eye, to communicate respectfully and clearly.

Over the years, it has become a common observation that homeschooled children are often much more confident and more interested in having a conversation with someone outside of their age group. This observation has less to do with homeschooling and more to do with the investment that these parents are making in their children and people of all different ages. They are communicating with their children, giving them opportunities to practice communicating with people of other ages, and purposefully preparing them for interacting respectfully in the world. The parents who have produced socially confident and courageous children have a few things in common. They have limited technology, provide face-to-face social experiences, teach their children to value all people, and how to respectfully speak with people of all ages.

Because social skills are becoming less common, those who have these skills will excel above the rest of their generation.

Social skills include:

- Speaking and communicating confidently.
- Actively listening.
- Asking thoughtful questions.
- Making eye contact.
- Being able to mediate in conflict and facilitate reconciliation.
- Having common social manners.
- Being aware of and understanding non-verbal body language.
- How to pay attention to timing in communication; when to hold back and when to say something.
- Paying attention to the room with an eye towards helping others feel comfortable and engaging those who may be feeling left out.
- How to share constructive feedback with others in a way they will listen to it.

These skills are crucial for those who desire to influence their generation and communities, regardless of the profession they pursue. These skills will also be invaluable for getting accepted into popular programs, higher education, getting hired for a job or apprenticeship, meeting with a future spouse's parents, integrating into society, and defending their faith to all people, to name a few.

Parenting QUESTIONS

- ❖ Are you providing opportunities for your children to practice conversing with adults and children of all ages respectfully and confidently?

- Do you value your children's opinions and invite them into your discussions when appropriate?
- Are you in a community, or cultivating a community, where people value talking with your child? Or do they brush them aside because they are young?
- Do your children segregate who they will play with into age groups, or can they play with children older and younger than them?
- Do your children understand necessary social graces, such as what is acceptable and unacceptable regarding interruptions (social rudeness), have a sense of understanding when things are funny and when they are not (social awkwardness), and how to graciously accept a compliment, and even observe body language cues of discomfort regarding what is a comfortable distance to stand next to someone else while talking?
- Do your children tend to think selfishly in groups of people, or are they socially aware and have a servant's heart, contributing in a way that makes the social event a good experience for everyone?

Courageous Parenting CHALLENGE

- Evaluate how your children interact in society. Are they confident, overly talkative, timid, or scared?
- How do they interact with children their age?
- How much time do they spend being antisocial because of technology or other activities?

Set boundaries or add activities to push your child out of their comfort zone. Teaching social manners is a parent's duty that prepares them for real life.

PRAYER

Father, we understand that being able to communicate is a crucial skill that our children need to master. We also recognize that it could be easy for them to spend hours a day being antisocial or keeping to themselves. Please help us to use discretion in setting boundaries and to be creative in how to challenge our children by getting social practice with people of all ages. Lord, we want to parent our child to be a light in the world more than anything, and we realize that any selfish disobedience, purposeful rudeness, poor body language, and even comments that they might make in social settings could cause conflict and hurt others' feelings. Father, please help us to teach and train our children to be ambassadors for you in this dark world.

For Your Glory, Amen.

CHAPTER 22

Differentiating Life Skills

It may seem obvious to you that your children need to be taught basic home economics, but it's a shocking truth that many children launch from their homes and don't know how to do their laundry, keep up a home, shop for or cook healthy foods, maintain basic automotive care, file taxes, let alone how to make homemade bread, calm a fussy baby and care for medical needs. I know this personally because we were two of those young adults.

When I, Angie, got married, boot camp began. I didn't know the first thing about home management, cooking, sewing, building a credit score, hospitality, home and car repairs, primary natural medicinal care for illnesses, handling insurance, or anything about sleep training, educating, or discipling a child!

If you don't train your child in these skills, they won't know either.

Now, some may argue that specific household duties should be taught to daughters over sons, or sons over daughters. That is for you and your husband to decide. We see a massive benefit in training both boys and girls in these essential life skills.

Because we don't fully know God's will for our children's lives, we must prepare them for both marriage and single adulthood. If a son doesn't get married until he is 30 years old, he should know how to cook, so he is not eating out regularly or failing to launch and spending every meal at mom and dad's home. Some might marry at a younger age, in which case we should want them to be a blessing to their spouse.

There have been seasons in our marriage, like when I was on bed rest, when my husband had to take care of necessary home management details around the home, like cooking and laundry. I grew in a strong conviction then that I wanted my sons to be prepared to care for their families if their wives cannot at some point.

I want to make sure our children all feel confident in marriage readiness by the time they leave our home. When my husband and I gave our daughters' hands in marriage, I wanted to feel confident that I had done my best in preparing them in both the spiritual and practical aspects of friendship, family, marriage, and home management.

If you have small children, teaching home economics starts as soon as they are mobile. Begin with teaching essential tidiness and organizational skills. Teach and hold your toddler accountable for putting a toy away before getting another one out. Let your little children help sort laundry, wash loads by colors, fold, and put clothing away. On a side note, it also encourages learning their primary colors.

Involving your children in your most basic household chores will take patience on your part. Teaching children under eight years old new skills like loading the dishwasher and how to sweep effectively can either be a fun adventure or one where you wind up frustrated, yelling, and redoing all their hard work. Choose the fun, adventurous attitude. It is crucial to prepare your heart attitude when you are teaching a new skill. Realistic expectations can make it or break it. You will need to choose to have patience and grace with your child. You don't want to discourage them from learning from you, and you don't want to discourage them from doing the chore! Even if they don't do it up to your standards, it is important to affirm and praise them for the work they did do! It builds their confidence, and they will be more likely to want to continue helping with a good, happy heart, as we say.

Be encouraged that once you do train them, and it only takes a little while, it will reap a harvest in your children. They will have learned life skills, and they can now begin being a part of the family team and doing "their part," which will fulfill their need for a sense of contribution. Every person, regardless of their age, wants to feel like they are needed and are contributing. Prepare your child to contribute to the family, and they will thrive.

Self-Defense & Survival Skills

The reality is that we don't know what to expect in our child's future or ours. However, we do know what the Bible says regarding end times:

"As he sat on the Mount of Olives, the disciples came to him privately, saying, 'Tell us, when will these things be, and what will be the sign of your coming and of the end of the age?" And Jesus answered them, "See that no one leads you astray. For many will come in my name, saying, 'I am the Christ,' and they will lead many astray. And you will hear of wars and rumors of wars. See that you are not alarmed, for this must take place, but the end is not yet. For nation will rise against nation, and kingdom against kingdom, and there will be famines and earthquakes in various places. All these are but the beginning of the birth pains.

"Then they will deliver you up to tribulation and put you to death, and you will be hated by all nations for my name's sake. And then many will fall away[a] and betray one another and hate one another. And many false prophets will arise and lead many astray. And because lawlessness will be increased, the love of many will grow cold. But the one who endures to the end will be saved. And this gospel of the kingdom will be proclaimed throughout the whole world as a testimony to all nations, and then the end will come." Matthew 24: 3-14

It would be advantageous for us to begin a new legacy, starting with our children, of knowing how to defend ourselves and the weak. There may come a time when self-defense and survival skills are needed. If these skills are not necessary for our lifetime, possibly our children will need them in theirs?

We believe it's no longer an optional, novel idea to make sure your children have confidence in protecting themselves. Self-defense should be viewed similarly to swimming; it's an essential life-or-death skill that should be mandatory to a certain degree. We aren't recommending a specific discipline in self-defense, but it's something we've invested in with our children.

Additionally, we would also advocate for teaching how to use a firearm and take care of it with ongoing practice as they get older. If you don't have experience with this, others around you probably do, and it's never too late to learn. Some higher-end shooting ranges provide training, and you can even rent their weapons while you are there, too.

The reality is that we cannot protect our children from every ill-willed offender. Our children need to be equipped with the necessary self-defense skills to be able to defend themselves and our grandchildren one day.

Today's children are, for the majority, very ill-equipped in survival skills and even have a basic understanding of how to provide and care for themselves if an emergency were to occur. We have found in raising our nine children that when you choose to start embarking on teaching and learning life skills with your children, the benefits to life far outweigh any sacrifices. In fact, you will most likely experience your children "coming alive" and passionate about new hobbies or areas of study, and it's incredibly life-giving to find something of interest to be passionate about. Another reality we have experienced is that when you allow your life to move in a direction that allows room for lifestyle choices that will incorporate needing to work at caring for livestock, or growing one's own food, for example, then the issue of wanting to teach work ethic is also solved, along with learning new life skills! Education becomes lifelong learning, and then the door to learning anything becomes open and contagious within your family culture!

Survival skills can also include but are not limited to knowing how to chop wood, start a fire, hunt, fish, skin a chicken, process meat, trap mice, plant a garden and harvest it, preserve vegetables, change a flat tire or the oil in a vehicle, basic building and household repair experience, manage finances, negotiate purchases, install a fence, weld, sew, make and use natural and herbal remedies, how to fix basic plumbing and electrical issues, basic home repairs, and drive big rigs or stick shifts.

Parenting QUESTIONS

- ❖ On a scale of 1-5, one being not at all, and five being pretty focused, how well are you doing at equipping your children with home economics and self-defense/survival skills? If you haven't been teaching your children any of these skills, why not?
- ❖ Out of the list of home economics skills listed, which ones do you need to be more intentional about teaching to your children? What other skills do you and your spouse deem necessary to know that we have not listed here?
- ❖ Have you had conversations with your children about awareness and not being distracted by devices when in public places? Are they aware of the realities of the world and understand the importance of discerning when something feels off or unsafe? Lastly, do they have the bravery to speak up, leave, say no, and make wise choices to protect themselves?

Courageous Parenting CHALLENGE

- ❖ Do you see the importance of teaching your children these skills?
- ❖ How motivated are you to start?
- ❖ Make a plan for what you are going to teach (weekly, monthly, or yearly). Let your children know that you intend to teach them and to get them ready for being an adult! Ask them what they would like to learn first. If it is something you don't know, find someone who can teach you together, or your child.

Remember, you don't have to be the one who teaches them everything. Look for mentors who can help in your family and Church community.

Courageous Parenting PODCAST

- Raising Kids Who are Resourceful and Take Initiative (Ep. 64)

PRAYER

Father, we know that the work we do in our homes, serving our families, brings You glory. Please help us to be patient in teaching our children. We do want to help them to be ready for marriage and adult life. We understand that You have a plan and purpose for our child's life that goes beyond them living in our homes, and that we have been given a great task to partner with you in preparing them! Thank You for this incredible opportunity and mission to be able to teach our children what we have learned over the years. Please help us to have the enthusiasm and to be able to motivate them and appreciate them as they learn how to help more. Please help us let go of tasks we are used to doing, and help us be more flexible in how things get accomplished. Help us to have a grateful heart attitude as our children grow in helpfulness.

In Jesus' Name We Pray, Amen.

CHAPTER 23

Biblical Financial Perspectives

I don't know a parent on the face of the planet that wouldn't want their child to have financial success, but our primary concern in this area should be that they have a biblical worldview of money and success, not that they would achieve a certain goal.

We don't know our children's future, but we should trust God with our children and surrender them and their futures back into His hands. We don't know if our children will be wealthy or struggle financially in their lives, but we should be preparing them to have a biblical relationship with money so that God can trust them, either way, and so they can be used by God for His glory.

> *"For where your treasure is, there your heart will be also."*
>
> Matthew 6:21

> *"If then you have not been faithful in the unrighteous wealth, who will entrust to you the true riches?"*
>
> Luke 16:11

Our children need to have a biblical understanding of God's economy.

First of all, we need to teach our children how we can honor God with the money he provides as a resource for us. We must teach our children that money is a neutral thing, just like any resource that can be used for noble or selfish purposes. Our human judgments can get in the way of a lot in life. We should not judge that someone with money is greedy (poverty gospel), nor should we assume that someone who is not wealthy must have some sin in their life (prosperity gospel), preventing God's blessing. Many extreme beliefs are tossed around in the Christian culture regarding money. We need to make sure that our children view this resource biblically, and that they know how to guard themselves against lust, covetousness, or discontentment, along with any other temptations of the heart, since that is what God cares about. Also, we must warn our children against the sins of idleness and entitlement.

It's important to realize that children grow up with different expectations for what a good amount of money is to earn. That expectation helps form their standard of money and resources.

It's also true that people often achieve at the level of their expectations of what they will earn someday. Expectations have a huge impact on their future earning potential.

So how do you navigate this? Well, we don't want unrealistic expectations that crush building towards a future or cause discontentment when your daughter gets married. We also don't want to unintentionally create an artificial ceiling on their future earning potential, either.

People often achieve at the level of their expectations of what they will earn someday.

We've attempted to raise our children in a way that doesn't cast a ceiling on earning in their minds, but at the same time doesn't cause discontentment with an average income either. This is important as we don't know what they're called to do yet or who they will marry. You'd rather they go in the direction of their natural gifting and callings than make a financial target the focus, regardless of whether it goes against who they are.

You'd also hate for your daughters to miss the right person to marry or for her to put undue pressure on a young man because she has some kind of lifestyle target in her mind that's unreasonable.

This takes purposeful effort to cultivate the balance in their minds as they grow up. Do your marriage and family conversations influence a healthy, balanced perspective on future earning potential?

Do your children see ways to earn money that are different from your experiences in life? Do you discuss financial principles and news as part of your table talk? Do business problems and ideas stir dialogue as your children get older? Do you share candidly what things cost, how your family's income or revenue comes in, the challenges, and the great opportunities as well?

We know that in this life, people experience trials of various kinds, and one of those kinds is financial turmoil. How can we equip our children so that they might avoid an unnecessary economic crisis?

Seven Biblical Money Management Principles to Teach Your Children:

1. Avoid consumer debt. Romans 13:8
2. Wealth gained hastily will dwindle. Proverbs 13:11
3. Seek wise counsel. Proverbs 11:14
4. Invest Wisely. Matthew 25:14-30
5. Be Frugal and Prudent. Proverbs 19:14, John 6:12
6. Save wisely and invest in being prepared. Proverbs 31:25
7. Give generously through caring for the needy and tithing. 2 Cor. 9:7, Luke 6:38, Acts 20:35

Chores vs. Contributions and Commissions

Over the years, we have evaluated the pros and cons of giving an allowance, and we have come to the conclusion that giving an allowance without any work attached leaves children prone to having an entitlement attitude towards money. Just give it to me for being here;

I deserve it without doing anything. The real world and economy do not work this way, so we have chosen not to pay for chores, although we do pay for commission jobs. And then we teach our children principles about money with what they earn from commission jobs. This is partially because we believe that children should be taught to steward their things, care for their rooms, and make their beds, for example, not because they will be paid for it but because it is good stewardship. Now, if we hired one of our children to do something that is not within their jurisdiction, then we can choose to pay them a commission! The point is that within a healthy home, you have members of a family all contributing and taking care of their jurisdictions together or simultaneously, which leads to a well-managed home.

Your children must actually experience managing their money properly while living in your home in these four areas:

1. Giving
2. Investing
3. Saving
4. Spending

Here's an example of how we've done this

Over the years, we have done this through a host of different ways. One year, we got little bird houses from a local craft store, enough for each child to have three unique houses that represented a home, a church, and a bank. The children all painted the house and nailed it to their own boards, and each divided up their money into the different bird houses to teach them the importance of spending, saving, investing, and giving. We had them put investing and savings in the same house, which represented the bank, because the project got large with all the houses.

We need to begin teaching our children how to view God's money as soon as they start earning it! We can do this best by helping them to practice the spiritual disciplines of managing God's money as they begin earning from hard work.

To continue the value of their experience, our children would delight in putting their giving in sandwich bags to give it at church. Additionally, they would set goals for something they were saving up for, and give them wisdom as they used their money for things.

One of the great conversations to have with a young child who has worked hard for their own money is to help them see the value of their dollars. Let's say your son wants to spend $20 on a toy truck.

Figure out how many hours it took him to make the $20, let's say it's six hours, and ask the question: "Son, before you purchase, I want you to think about something; it took you six hours to make the money that this truck costs, is this toy truck worth the six hours of work it took you to save for it?"

BOOM!! Whether he says yes or no, it's a win. You have elevated his thought process about spending wisely and the value of his time and money.

Teach the principle of building assets vs. buying liabilities.

This is vital in a future where robots will be taking over so many things. Your children need to understand the importance of building assets such as real estate, businesses, and other investments.

Assets versus liabilities

- Assets help you create value and/or pay you money that's not tied to your direct labor.
- Liabilities depreciate and cost you money.

Here's an example of two 12-year-old children:

Child A saves up money and buys a pretty sweet bike. He gets his bike and enjoys it immensely at first, but its use wanes over time, and so does its value.

Child B uses the same amount of money to buy a lawn mower and a weed eater. He then uses those business assets to serve his neighborhood by mowing their lawns for a fee. In the first month, he got his money back, and now he's making a profit by leveraging his assets. At the end of the summer, he has enough money to buy three bikes like child A, plus he owns his business assets.

But he doesn't want to buy a new bike; instead, he wants to ride the old one and invest some of his money, so it starts working for him because he understands the importance of cultivating leveraged revenue. Revenue that's created, but not tied to his direct labor.

All the learning, experience, and growth he's gone through to run a little business will serve him throughout his life because it has also built confidence.

Which child is yours?

The one source of income plan where it's tied to someone's direct labor is a more risky direction than it's ever been before. In the future, we believe your children must develop multiple sources of income, at least some of which aren't directly tied to their labor.

Your children must cultivate more resilient ways to earn than people have had to in previous generations. Giving them inspiration and helping them exercise the muscle of dreaming and building something, whether a product or a service, will be one of the most powerful experiences in their childhood.

Keep your children informed about changes in finance as they develop as well.

We live in an age where all of this is changing before our eyes. If your children don't understand cryptocurrency as they get older, it will become a disadvantage for them.

Preparing Children to Handle Financial Hardships

Nothing is guaranteed in this life, except the faithfulness of our God, and that is more than enough. Your son might be wealthy one day and lose it all the next. It is crucial that, in teaching children about money, we remind them not to take it for granted but to have grateful hearts. Remember, God cares about our character and hearts above all else. And He will discipline those He loves. We do not want to provoke God to test us.

Angie's testimony

While we were engaged, we were building a business together, but shortly after getting married, I became pregnant with our first child, and my role changed drastically. I became the support from the home front. Isaac has been self-employed his entire adult life, providing much fruit and adventure as he has built several successful companies, but at age forty, right after birthing our seventh child, he had to close his company with forty-three employees, and we lost everything financially. Failure is not an easy pill to swallow, and neither is the financial strain on a marriage and family. Though our world values success more than failure, God cares most about how we handle both. What do our character and integrity look like in abundance and in hardship? You can work hard, but it does not guarantee success. So, how do you handle the stress of the financial consequences that follow a failed business?

- Do you grow closer to God or farther away?
- Do you honor Him as you pursue debtors, or do you hide?
- Do you fight to get out of debt and have a teachable, joyful heart attitude along the way?
- Are you humble when you are succeeding?
- Do you only value the knowledge of the successful, or do you pursue the knowledge and understanding of one who has suffered and failed? Hindsight is full of wisdom.
- Ultimately, the question is, will you walk in faith and make decisions in His wisdom, or will you make decisions from your own human wisdom and strength?

Have you suffered a loss or walked through financial struggles? What did your children witness? Did you seek God more, and did your attitude reflect that of a person trusting God or one who is doing it all in his strength and getting exhausted doing it?

If you have, I encourage you to find the lessons in your experience and be open with your children about it. Let them, as much as possible, learn from your mistakes. If your children can understand what is going on as you walk through hard financial times, let them see you praise God through it. Model for them gratefulness and someone who "count it all joy, my brothers, when you meet trials of various kinds." James 1:1

It is in these moments that our children see our faith in action. When they see us relying on God for the provision and praising Him, they will later recall these moments as some of the most molding teaching examples of their lives.

Don't rob your children of witnessing God coming through, because you're fearful of being fully transparent with your children. That fear is prompted by pride. You will need their prayers, and it will show spiritual strength in your family if they see you responding in faith in the moments where nothing in your strength will work.

As you experience trials, engage them, ask God, "What lesson are you teaching me?" Then share it with your family! It will bless them and build a strong legacy of faith.

And if you haven't yet experienced financial struggles, praise the Lord!

Remember to model generosity to your children and involve them in the decision-making process of who you are going to bless and share with your family about your tithes and offerings, too.

They are part of the family unit, and it's powerful when they see your faith in action when it comes to finances. Teach them about how God is the giver of all you have. Remind them that it is His, and your desire for Him to be able to continue to trust you. You have been given an incredible gift! Don't bury your talents, but steward them well. Build treasures in Heaven, my friend, and invite your children to witness it, do it with you, and experience the heart transformation that can come from being generous.

Parenting QUESTIONS

- Do you model good spending habits for your children?
- Do you tend to stress over money issues regularly? If so, what do you think that is teaching your children?
- Have you walked through a hard time financially? How did you respond? What did your children witness? How could you have purposefully redeemed that trial to bring God glory in the midst of it?
- Do your children have a biblical perspective on money?
- Are you teaching your children how to manage money?

Courageous Parenting CHALLENGE

Evaluate your children:

- Have they typically enjoyed instant gratification (spoiling) or have they learned joy and contentment? Choose a form of delayed gratification that you can use to teach your children the value of money.
- What ways can you help your children understand the value of a dollar? Come up with a job they can do for commission and then teach them the basic principles of saving, investing, tithing (giving), and spending.

Here are some key Scriptures to use in teaching your children more biblical principles regarding money:

Six Ways We Know We Can Honor God with Our Money

1. Meet the needs of our family. (1 Timothy 5:8)
2. Graciously give to those in need. (Lev. 25:35-37)
3. Delight in the blessings He provides us with a grateful heart. (Phil. 4:11-13; 1 Tim. 6:6-12)

4. Give the Elders Double Honor, especially those who labor in word. (1 Tim. 5:17)
5. Build treasures in Heaven .(Matthew 6:19-20 & Malachi 3:8-10)
6. Leave an inheritance for your children. (Proverbs 13:22)

Courageous Parenting PODCAST

- How to Parent Through Life Trials & Financial Struggles (Ep. 5)

PRAYER

Lord, Your Word warns us that the LOVE of money is the root of all evil. We know money isn't evil, but please guard us all against lusting after things of this world. May Your Spirit cultivate in our hearts contentment with what you have given us today? Help us to raise wise children who steward the blessings and talents you give them well. Might their dealings and ours glorify you? May you bless our families so that we can be a blessing to others and build treasures in Heaven. Lord, more than anything, we want our children to value building treasures in heaven, but we know that is something that only Your Holy Spirit can impress on someone's heart, so we ask that our children would get that concept! We pray our children will use the gifts you give them to further Your Kingdom.

In Jesus Name, Amen.

SECTION THREE

Marriage Challenge

Begin your date night in prayer together. Evaluate the previous chapters topics below and discuss any areas that you might be out of alignment or need to develop a plan together on as you parent as a team.

PRAYER

Father God, please protect our marriage right now as we attempt to discuss topics regarding our parenting. We want to bring You glory in our marriage and parenting and ask You to lead us. May our family be a beacon of light in this world. Give us wisdom and insight in the decisions we need to make, and please soften our children's hearts to want to be like You and obey Your word. In Jesus' Name, Amen.

Here are the sections of Chapter Three to discuss:

The Skills for Thriving

- Design & Influence Your Family Culture
- Producers Versus Consumers
- Social Media, Gaming, & Internet Access
- Christian Parenting in an AI World
- Work Ethic & Integrity Vs. Entitlement

- Social Awareness & Communication Skills
- Differentiating Life Skills
- Biblical Financial Perspectives

Courageous Parenting CHALLENGE

Take a moment to dream with your spouse about what you desire for your future. What has God put on your heart to pray for and work towards regarding family relationships, family culture, closeness, etc., in the next 10, 20, and 30 years? Dream about holidays, vacations, where you live, and your legacy. What is God calling you to?

Spend some time writing out what God has placed on your heart for the future. Then, below that, identify and write out key things that need to change and need to continue to grow in order for you to reach your vision for your family.

One example we can share is that we dreamt of our kids all living fairly close to one another, and in each other's lives. While we have been preparing our hearts that it would be a pipe dream for all nine of our children, and we are preparing our hearts for that, we chose to move to a state and an area that would align the most closely with biblical truth, freedom, and political likemindedness in hopes that our children would value that and make their decisions wisely for their legacy and generations before them. That is an example of a BIG change.

Other smaller yet just as powerful examples would be in choosing what church to build community and put roots down in, what educational choices will be the best for the outcome you are desiring and valuing the most. Maybe there is a need to make some changes to technology because you are sensing your child is literally changing for the worse, the more time they spend on devices. Whatever your vision or dream is, there are action steps you can identify that can help you move your family towards that vision.

Write them out, pray together about them, and when the time comes, share them with your family.

SECTION 04

Spiritual Maturity & Battle Ready

CHAPTER 24

Discipled for Wise Decision Making

There is no doubt our children will have BIG decisions ahead of them. As parents, we don't realize how easy we have it when they live at home and have some amount of control concerning who their friends are, what their bedtime is, what they eat, what they learn, etc. Then one day, they have grown up, and they are pursuing a job opportunity, starting a business, getting married, buying a car or home, and deciding where to live. There are so many choices our children get to make, and we need to let and encourage them to make them wisely.

Blessed is the parent who can say to her daughter or son, "I trust you will make a wise decision." That should be our goal: to help our children develop wise decision-making skills, to witness their excellent decisions up close and personal, and to then trust that God will guide them and that they will listen.

We must cultivate the type of relationship that we desire to have with our children while they are young. If we think that our children will just come to us for advice because we are their parents, we are sadly mistaken. Firstly, we have to be the type of person they want advice from. Secondly, we must develop a relationship with our children where they come to us for advice. We are, after all, the guidance counselors and discipleship trainers God chose for our children.

We are qualified in Christ. However, once they are older and do come to us for advice, we should continue to confidently lead them to a dependency on Christ, not a co-dependency on us. We must encourage our children to seek Him and His Word for His will.

We should want our children to live out God's will for their lives.

Have you ever thought about how there are different types of wisdom? There is biblical wisdom, which is God's wisdom, based on the truth in His Word. Worldly wisdom, in contrast to biblical wisdom, is frequently at odds with God's Word. Then there is a form of wisdom that is often characterized by age, but comes from hindsight. We all know that just because someone is old, it doesn't make them wise. To have wisdom in old age requires humility and introspection; an ability to look at one's life through a clear and objective lens, looking for lessons learned.

The world has seeped into so many Christians' perspectives, regardless of age, so it's important to teach your children how to discern if someone's wisdom is worthy. Here are some questions you can teach to your children:

- Is it grounded in biblical truth?
- Are they walking strong with the Lord?
- Is there fruit in their life?
- Did they truly listen to understand?
- Is there a potential agenda behind the wisdom they are giving?

It's important for your children to get wisdom from others and experience that as they get older in your home, but it's getting harder to find people who will actually give sound wisdom. You should tell your children this and continually teach them how to discern when to listen to the words of another on important matters.

One of the things we do with our children to help them with situations where they had a conversation with someone where they weren't sure if it went well or not is to have a conversation about the conversation. This is a key ingredient in intentional parenting. The most intentional parents we have met over the years have had the type of relationship with their children where they are able to dialogue and teach in real-time friendship scenarios.

For example, asking "What did he share with you, son?" and "What did you say next?" and so forth. Role playing, to play it out and look for whether your child is just following, or really discerning whether what someone is saying is sound or not, is important. When you find they are discerning and leading, encourage them, tell them you trust them, and affirm their wisdom. If they are not leading, encourage them to do so or to make wise choices in friends. In other cases, children may seek advice by going through it with us because they sense something off and can't fully tell, so they want wise counsel. Then there are the times when they are excited to share how they stood firm for what's right and discuss it with us. At times, other children are there listening to (If it's appropriate to do so) and learning.

This is often in the evening after our littles go to sleep, and an older (or many older) comes into our bedroom and sits on the couch to chat. Rich times where wisdom is reinforced through real situations.

Here are four things to do to help your children make wise choices:

1. Invest time in memorizing scripture (specifically Proverbs and Psalms) with children when they are young. Proverbs is called wisdom literature for a reason. There is no better wisdom than God's.
2. Let them practice making decisions while they are under your roof. If you make all their decisions for them, they will not have had to make any decisions before and experience the consequences of those decisions when they are much less harsh. So let them make bad choices and let them suffer the consequences.
3. Teach your children the process of making a wise decision. When you are discipling them or just having discussions, share with them how and why you are making the decisions

you are making. Teach them the thinking process you go through in choosing. For example, if you and your husband were thinking of starting a business or buying a home, you can model for your children the process that you follow in making a wise decision. Model for them praying about it, seeking wise counsel from a mentor, elder, or even one of your parents. You also want to model for your children, making decisions in alignment as a married couple.

4. Pray HARD! Pray they remember the scripture you worked hard to help them memorize, pray they exercise that wisdom in their decision-making, and pray that God will guard and guide them. Psalm 119:9

We must disciple our children to know God's Word and see Him as the author of wisdom, but to also have a humble heart that regularly looks to learn from their mistakes and others.

Parenting QUESTIONS

- Do you model-wise decision-making?
- Have you been transparent with your children about how you make decisions?
- Have you allowed them to make choices and fail?
- Have you taught them how to make wise choices?

Courageous Parenting CHALLENGE

Try to think of something you could let your child do to give them more freedom in decision-making. As they make wise decisions, affirm them and recognize why it was a wise decision. When they make an unwise decision, like choosing to disobey you, remind them when you are disciplining them that they made an unwise choice and they disobeyed the wisdom in God's Word. Again, try changing your vocabulary to use wise/unwise rather than bad or good. We want our children to be making wise decisions, not just good ones.

Courageous Parenting PODCAST

- Helping Your Kids Grow in Maturity (Ep. 185)
- Are You Paralyzing Your Kids' Spiritual Growth (Ep. 13)

PRAYER

Father, Your wisdom is higher than any of man's wisdom. Would you give each of us your understanding as we parent our children? Please help us to allow them the opportunity to be stretched and grow in making wise decisions while they are in our homes. Please help us have self-control over protecting them from all of the consequences that can come from foolish decisions, so that they can experience the real pain that can come from making unwise choices. We pray that, above all, our children would make wise decisions regarding the friends they choose. We pray they understand that the friends they choose will have an impact on their lives. May Your will be done in our child's life.

Thank you, Lord, Amen

CHAPTER 25

Trained in Weapons of Righteousness

The Bible warns us that if we don't exercise self-control, then we will become slaves to whatever controls us.

One of the most important character qualities and spiritual disciplines you could pass on to your children is the ability to exercise self-control. It will radically change the course of your child's future, not to mention bless their future relationships and legacy. But above any human ability for self-control, we must also remember that self-control is a fruit of the Spirit.

"But the fruit of the Spirit is love, joy, peace, patience, kindness, goodness, faithfulness, gentleness, self-control; against such things there is no law." Galatians 5:22-23

We cannot expect our children to exercise the spirit-filled fruit of self-control if they are not born again. Having realistic expectations is incredibly important as we parent children, discipling them towards Jesus and walking with longsuffering, patiently with them on their own personal journey of spiritual growth with the Lord. This evaluation applies to everyone you know who doesn't "walk by the spirit." It's helpful to be able to have understanding and compassion for those who don't know Jesus and His Word, or haven't been regenerated.

Here's an easier said than done reality: you cannot just read to your child about self-control and expect them to exercise it in their own strength without wavering. Another thing that we have said redundantly is that we must model for our children what God's word teaches and what we are teaching and expecting of them.

As we said before, children are hypocrite hounds, and if you are going to expect self-control, you should also be prepared to practice it yourself in front of them.

> *"A man without self-control is like a city broken into and left without walls."*
>
> Prov. 25:28

Any temptation of the flesh will need to be wielded by the power of the Spirit and the weapon of self-control. Your child will undoubtedly be tempted by many men and women, in many different circumstances, and in different ways. If you train your child how to be self-controlled in both their actions as well as their responses and reactions to others, they will be far better off. The person who has no self-control can get themselves into a lot of trouble in relationships.

God's word is full of warnings regarding relationships. We studied a few of them in other chapters. Imagine someone who doesn't have self-control regarding their temper or tongue?

"Know this, my beloved brothers: let every person be quick to hear, slow to speak, slow to anger; for the anger of man does not produce the righteousness of God. Therefore, put away all filthiness and rampant wickedness and receive with meekness the implanted word, which is able to save your souls." James 1:19-21

"But avoid irreverent babble, for it will lead people into more and more ungodliness," 2 Tim. 2:16

"Keep your tongue from evil and your lips from speaking deceit." Psalm 34:13

"Let no corrupting talk come out of your mouths, but only such as is good for building up, as fits the occasion, that it may give grace to those who hear." Eph. 4:29

"Do not speak evil against one another, brothers. The one who speaks against a brother or judges his brother speaks evil against the law and judges the law. But if you judge the law, you are not a doer of the law but a judge." James 4:11

"If anyone thinks he is religious and does not bridle his tongue but deceives his heart, this person's religion is worthless." James 1:26

"Besides that, they learn to be idlers, going about from house to house, and not only idlers, but also gossips and busybodies, saying what they should not." 1 TIm. 5:13

Doing a study on the power of the tongue and God's warnings to those with loose lips is found in the word of God. Teaching our children to be wise and slow to speak will be one of the most powerful skills in their lives. Proverbs 2:11 says,

> "Discretion will watch over you, understanding will guard you…"

When it comes to self-control, there are many things God calls us to exercise self-control over; the tongue is just one example of many. For example, having self-control over emotions or a temper is one that many parents can focus on with younger children. If you begin teaching and training this from a young age, parenting will be significantly easier when children grow up into their teen years. To this day, one of my children's ears perk up when I say the phrase self-control because they heard it so frequently as a child. And you would never guess that specific child had struggled with temper tantrums as a toddler because they have such a peaceful countenance. But again, when it comes to teaching a character quality like self-control over emotions, you can expect what you are not modeling yourself.

Parenting QUESTIONS

- ❖ Do you struggle with self-control over your tongue or temper?
- ❖ Do your children struggle with their tongue or temper? Evaluate each child.
- ❖ When you are training your children, do you use the word *self-control*?
- ❖ What are some areas you can pinpoint in your child's life where you could begin holding them accountable for having self-control?

Courageous Parenting CHALLENGE

If you have sinned against anyone in your family and lacked self-control, we urge you to apologize and ask for forgiveness.

Then begin the conversation about being spiritually disciplined and having self-control, whether that be over what you eat, how you clean your home, not speaking about others, not losing your temper, and discuss what it means to literally have control over yourself. When we are living and breathing by the word of God, we should desire spiritual disciplines such as self-control. Explain to your children how important it is to desire the Spirit, the ways of God, and to ask Him for those things. Then, if you don't already, begin changing the vocabulary in your home so that you use words such as "self-control" regularly. Once your children realize how often it is being brought up, they will understand just how important it is that they pursue it.

Courageous Parenting PODCAST

- Dealing with Emotional Outbursts (Ep. 184)

PRAYER

God, thank you for giving us Your Spirit, that we might live in freedom from the slavery of those things that want to bind us. Would you bless us all as parents as we seek to have more self-control and train our children to do the same? We pray that your will would be done in all our lives, and that as we seek to live in You, those shackles of bad habits would fall right off of us. We pray that our children would see a massive difference in their parents, and that they would want to be self-controlled too! We pray that you would give them self-control over their fleshly desires. Protect them from being influenced by others who have no self-control. Give them wisdom to seek friends that do exhibit this spiritual discipline, in Jesus holy Name, Amen.

CHAPTER 26

Help Their Respectfulness Rise

When you ask the older generations what's wrong with children today, they almost unanimously reply, "Children today have no respect for anyone or anything."

We all know that a lack of respect for others is usually spurred on by a lack of self-respect and a lack of respect or reverence for God. We live in an age when most who say they are Christian don't even believe what the Bible says, and many don't even claim to be a Christian. How can there be reverence for God when the people don't even believe He exists or His word?

Most of the painful heartache in this world can be traced back to two kinds of sin: selfishness and pride of mankind, and lack of respect or reverence.

If we want our children to have fruitful marriages and leave Faith-filled legacies, they must be respectful and have a sincere reverence for God.

Respect for God is developed as children witness their parents living out dedication and devotion to God. Every time they see mom or dad open the Bible and choose to put God first, they learn respect. When they witness their father studying and reading His word, praying to God, and trying to obey Him, they witness respect for God.

Just as boys learn respect for women by watching their dads respect their moms, they also learn respect for God by witnessing how their parents show respect to the Father in Heaven.

Here's a huge tip if you want more respect in your home: look for opportunities in the right moments to give respect to others even when they don't deserve it.

This is going to sound like it lacks justice to some of you, and certainly, you'd be right in some situations, but in the right situations, it's incredibly powerful and displays amazing leadership.

It's actually counterintuitive. Here's why it works: People rise to the level of respect you give to them. This is true in settings where the person giving the respect is admired and loved.

Your children will rise to a new level of respect you give them. How can you show your children more respect in certain situations? Watch them, they will rise to it!

Disobedience issues are common among families, schools, churches, and work environments today, but the problem doesn't end there.

Society is overrun with disrespectful citizens. Cursing, vandalism, squatting, foul language, road rage, anger outbursts to perfect strangers, and massive intolerance of basic human rights are just a few of the symptoms rampant in our society today. There seems to be hardly any respect for authority, or people's possessions or property, let alone human life!

We are raising children in a day and age when having biblical convictions can cost you your job, tarnish your reputation, and even worse, get you injured or killed.

We have to train our children on issues that were never meant to be political because they were a basic matter of reverence for life and biblical truth.

Our children will be more than pressured to switch sides on convictions like pro-life, gender, and the definition of marriage; they will be threatened. And if they aren't threatened, they will feel threatened and will become manipulated. Those who claim tolerance are often the most intolerant and even violent. They are untrustworthy, double-minded people.

If your children are young, the most important character quality you could focus on with them is respect. Respect is reflected in obedience and in the valuing and treatment of others' possessions, reputations, time, resources, feelings, opinions, and physical bodies. Teach your children that everyone is created and loved by God, that Jesus died for them all. And show respect to your children, your spouse, your parents, and authorities in your life. They learn it from you.

If your children are older, it is never too late to begin focusing on respect. Do not tolerate deliberate disrespect to anyone, but especially authority. Make sure your child is respectful to his friend's parents, teachers, pastors, policemen, etc. Remind your child that respect is visible in attitudes as well as actions. Encourage your child to be active in practicing respect by how they treat their own possessions, how they treat others' possessions, and their own attitude towards possessions.

And remember that your child will become like who he/she hangs out with. Be careful what friends you allow him to spend time with. Are they disrespectful? Being mean, sarcastic, teasing and cutting other people down should also never be allowed. Make sure that your child is not developing bad habits and a disrespectful character trait.

Parenting QUESTIONS

- ❖ Are your children respectful or disrespectful?
- ❖ What evidence do you see of them being respectful?
- ❖ What is their reputation regarding respectfulness in your community?

Courageous Parenting CHALLENGE

If you haven't focused on respect in your child training, now is the time to get REALLY serious about it. Start holding your child accountable for being disrespectful, and if "respect" isn't a part of your family's daily conversation, add it to your vocabulary. This is GO time! There is no time to spare on training in righteousness.

Courageous Parenting PODCAST

- How to Raise Kids Who Respect Their Parents(Ep. 4)
- How to Handle Disrespect: 4 Actionable Tips (Ep. 289)

PRAYER

Father, we know one of the chief purposes of man is to glorify You and enjoy You forever. We are aware that if we don't instill respect in our children, they will not bring You glory. We desire for our children to have a successful marriage and relationships with their siblings, children, and friends, and we know that teaching them the importance of being respectful is key to their personal success in relationships. But more importantly, if they have a deep reverent respect for you, a fear of God, then all these other desires for them will follow. Your word says, seek first the Kingdom of God and all these things will be added unto you. Give us wisdom and strength to be diligent and consistent in this. We know a lot is riding on teaching and instilling reverence for You, Your Son, and Your Holy Word. May Your Spirit richly dwell in our hearts and homes and help us to have that deep reverence for you. May our children experience it as we care for them.

To You Be the Glory. Amen.

CHAPTER 27

Cultivate a Hunger for Learning

Here are two questions to consider as we begin this chapter: Do you love learning?

Do your children love learning? What do your children perceive of you regarding continually learning and having a teachable heart?

As you think about each of your children and evaluate if they love learning, I first want you to distinguish between your child's interests (there may be different topics that they love learning more than others) and their attitude towards learning in general.

Take a moment to jot down your children's names and reflect on each of their heart attitudes towards learning. Do they get excited to learn new things, ask a lot of questions, and show a deep curiosity about life? Or do they seem bored, uninterested, and even distracted from figuring things out and desiring to be entertained?

Remember, a love for learning is something caught, not taught.

If your children witness you taking time to slow down, read, journal, and so forth, or even take a class here and there, and they see you delighting in it, they will witness a love for learning.

This is a culture you can cultivate in your family, but it takes intentionality, patience, and vision.

Regardless of whether your child loves learning or not, one of the most crucial lessons you need to instruct your child to understand is how to discern and use wisdom in WHAT he/she is learning and from whom.

Educational Choices Have Consequences

Let's talk about where children are being indoctrinated 40 hours per week.

As humans, we are constantly learning and growing, but we have the freedom to choose what we learn, how we learn it, and who we learn it from. Many good and well-intentioned teachers leave much more than an understanding of a subject of knowledge. They leave a perception of who created it, what it is meant for, and why it is important.

I prefer we speak as realists for a moment. While there are many good Christian teachers who are seeking to be missionaries in the government's education system, the truth is that for every one of them, there are twenty who view their role as an opportunity to indoctrinate children to be atheists, agnostics, or their own religious preferences. The truth is that all teachers know the power they wield, not just in your child's personal life, but also what that influence will yield in future generations. So be careful.

Don't be a negligent parent and just send them off to school without doing your research, knowing their teachers and peers, and what they are being taught.

Remember that you want a different-looking legacy, and you GET to dream, with the inspiration of the Holy Spirit, as to what that should be.

We live in the Age of Information, and your child is growing up in a culture where everyone goes to technology for answers and education. The point is that we have to teach our children to be as wise as serpents regarding who they allow to teach them and where they are getting their knowledge and information from.

Again, this is something that has to first be modeled in your life and home. Do you evaluate all teachers, curricula, books, movies, podcasts, seminars, and music through a biblical worldview and say no to things that are going to lead you astray, so to speak?

Do you evaluate your child's education and teach them to as well?

The truth is that the moment a parent signs a child up for a class with someone, they are subconsciously saying, **"I approve of this person and what they teach. Pay close attention, take good notes, learn from them, believe what they believe, and do what they say."**

As Christian parents, we need to be realists. We need to be willing to take an honest look at the agendas being taught and imposed upon our children, and we need to be willing to say, "This is not ok, I will not stand for it." If the school your child is attending is pushing anything that is against the Word of God and expecting them to tolerate blatant sin, it is a matter of time before your child will not agree with scripture or you.

A note to homeschool parents from Angie:

I want to exhort you regarding education as well. I have heard it said that "we don't focus so much on academia, we care more about character." This results in children being completely unprepared to leave their parents' homes and provide for a family of their own. I have also heard it said that "we homeschool to give our children a BETTER education." This argument also has its pitfalls, as many of those parents are more concerned about test scores and getting their child into a prestigious school, and in the end, they don't have much of a relationship with their child. Both of these extremes can produce performance-based learning and completely defeat the goal of love for learning.

I want to challenge you to find the happy harmony between both training in character and righteousness, and academia. It can be done.

Of course, when character fails, you drop the less eternal academics to focus on the heart issue at hand, but you don't give a free pass to finishing the work.

If you want to raise CONFIDENT COURAGEOUS children who love the Lord, are smart, and are going to make an impact in this world, you need to focus on both. Yes, it requires sacrifice and a lot of work, but this is where ministry happens as you disciple your children in all things.

Parenting QUESTIONS

- ❖ Do your children love learning? Do they realize their responsibility in protecting and guarding their minds from being deceived through different means of education?
- ❖ Are you evaluating their education, the teachers, and the peer environments surrounding their current educational experience?

Courageous Parenting CHALLENGE

Evaluate everything that educates your children and choose to set a standard of valuing biblical truth over what's popular, common, or easy.

This is going to be difficult. You may have to make some hard decisions, like not allowing your child to read that book they are assigned in Literature class, or even better, bring them home to educate them there.

Courageous Parenting PODCAST

- 11 Reasons Why We Homeschool Despite Initial Doubts (Ep. 35)
- Our 1st Generation Homeschooling Hardships & Blessings (Ep. 247)
- How Christians Should Evaluate Educational Choices (Ep. 16)

PRAYER

Father, we recognize that You are the great Teacher and that Your word has wisdom, instruction, teaching, and advice for everything in life. (2 Timothy 3:16) We understand that those who educate our children will have the power of influence in their lives and that will impact who they become as well as what they believe when they are older. Would You give us insight as to what we should do regarding our children's education? Give each of us strength, wisdom, courage, and perseverance to engage this issue head-on. Thank You for this awesome privilege of being a parent. We know You have called us to the role of teacher in our children's lives in Duet. 6. God, give us courage to be and do what You are asking us to do. Help us to seize the moment and season we have with our children. We desperately don't want to live with regrets and ask You to guide our marriages in the hard decisions we have to make as parents.

We live to know You and make You known, Jesus. Amen.

CHAPTER 28

Equipped for Spiritual Warfare

Spiritual warfare is real, and most parents don't teach or equip their children for this unspoken battle. We have been warned in Scripture about our enemy, the devil, in 1 Peter 5:8, and witness through Scriptural testimony how the enemy has attacked and influenced the persecution of followers of Christ. Jesus Himself encourages us to expect persecution (Matt. 5:9-11; Matt. 10:22; 1 Peter 4:12-19; Acts 5:41; Romans 8:17; 2 Cor. 1:7; 1 Peter 3:14). If Jesus teaches us to expect persecution, we should likewise prepare our children to expect it and show them how to handle it.

Just as the Holy Spirit comforts us through persecution, we should expect that there will be times we need to comfort our children as well.

If you are raising children who love Jesus and are pursuing holiness, you have a big target on your back, and so do your children. The enemy wants to discourage you from doing what you are called to do in raising your children purposefully in Jesus' name!

There are many Christians who don't like to talk about spiritual warfare. Christians who believe that the minute you speak of the devil is the moment you give him power. But that isn't how the devil gains power. We are being deceived if we think that he is more powerful by acknowledging his schemes. The truth is, if we recognize an attack for what it truly is, then we can respond in a Biblically appropriate and God-glorifying way and diffuse the enemy's plan. The minute we don't want to acknowledge spiritual attacks is the minute that we also miss an opportunity to train our children for spiritual battle. Not only that, but God has given us many scriptures that give us insight into the tactics of our enemy for the purpose of warning us and preparing us.

When one of our children began struggling with night terrors, as many call them. We knew it was a spiritual attack and refused to just blow it off as something normal that all kids experience, but instead prayed over our child and taught them the weapons of warfare to overcome the attack. Over the years, that response has served that child and many others well in overcoming the battle that would attempt to attack their mind. God gave us the weapons of righteousness and the armor of God for a reason. Equipping our children with the armor is one of the most powerful spiritual preparation methods they will ever gain. Memorizing Scripture and praying it in faith has a profound impact on both the battle itself, as we call upon the name of the Lord, as well as the faith of our children as they experience the power of God and His Holy Spirit in their lives.

> *"Working together with him, then, we appeal to you not to receive the grace of God in vain. For he says, 'In a favorable time I listened to you, and in a day of salvation I have helped you'"*
>
> 2 Cor. 6:1-2

Behold, now is the favorable time; behold, now is the day of salvation. We put no obstacle in anyone's way, so that no fault may be found with our ministry, but as servants of God we commend ourselves in every way: by great endurance, in afflictions, hardships, calamities, beatings, imprisonments, riots, labors, sleepless nights, hunger; by purity, knowledge, patience, kindness, the Holy Spirit, genuine love; by truthful speech, and the power of God; with the weapons of righteousness for the right hand and for the left; through honor and dishonor, through slander and praise." 2 Cor. 6:1-8

This passage of scripture immediately follows the Scripture in 2 Corinthians 5:16-20, where Paul is exhorting the church to recognize the power of the crucifixion and that we are made new in Christ, that we are now called ambassadors, and God makes his appeal through us and has given us this powerful ministry of reconciliation. When you recognize the incredible calling He has placed on our lives, as followers of God, and then we see him exhorting us not to take that grace in vain, but be ready with the weapons of righteousness, it brings a whole new meaning to this passage.

We must not neglect to teach our children that this is God's calling for them in Christ Jesus as well! This purpose brings meaning, purpose, mission, and vision to our lives! But also, we must prepare them for the reality of the adversity they will likely experience because of following Jesus!

If we, as Christ-followers, weren't called to fight the spiritual battle, why would God give us spiritual armor with which to fight? (Eph. 6)

There is too much evidence in the Bible that we, as Christians, will endure persecution and temptation from the world, the devil, and our fleshly nature. We must teach our children how to distinguish between these three enemies, and then we teach them how to respond Biblically.

If our children are like arrows in the hands of a mighty warrior, once they launch from our homes, they become warriors as well. As parents, we need to train them to fight the battle at hand in this generation. In combat training, soldiers are extensively trained in how to take apart their rifles and put them back together again. They repeatedly practice this skill to know their weapon as if it were an extension of themselves. As warriors fighting this spiritual battle, we need to know our weapons and teach our children how to use them.

"Above all, taking the shield of faith, wherewith ye shall be able to quench all the fiery darts of the wicked. And take the helmet of salvation, and the sword of the Spirit, which is the word of God." Ephesians 6:16-17

We must know the Word of God, as well as a soldier knows his gun.

Listen, we know we just opened a can of worms, so to speak, and that we're just brushing the surface here. But we think it is essential as parents, who are discipling their children and preparing them to be "in the world, but not of it" (Romans 12:1-2), that we absolutely must begin the discussion with our spouse about spiritual warfare. If we haven't already, we must start studying God's word regarding this, expect persecution because we are not living like the world, and know how to respond to it. Children must understand that spiritual warfare exists and that it's not something to play with, but rather to guard their hearts and minds against. If we allow our children to meddle in superstitions, new age movements, witchcraft, or even watch and read books with the occult in them in a way that appeals to learning to love and tolerate them, we are inviting the enemy into our homes and our children's hearts and minds. Let us be diligent gatekeepers of the hearts in our homes, protecting them and teaching them how to guard their minds and hearts in Christ Jesus.

Parenting QUESTIONS

- ❖ Do you believe in spiritual warfare? Have you and your children encountered a spiritual attack?
- ❖ Is this a topic that your children feel comfortable asking you about, discussing, and praying about together?
- ❖ Do you know your weapon? You really need to, because you can't teach what you don't know.

Courageous Parenting CHALLENGE

Speak with your husband about spiritual warfare. You are a team and need to consider your children's souls regarding what to teach them and when. If you are a parent of older children, we challenge you to be forthright in explaining all the Scripture and truth concerning spiritual warfare. Your children deserve and need to know the truth. We pray this chapter strikes a healthy fear that inspires action and the pursuit of God. You probably want more guidance concerning this topic, but here's an important reality you should take to heart: all you need for teaching on any of these topics is the Bible. It's God's guidebook for life and parenting!

After you discuss spiritual warfare with your spouse, decide what you both feel God is calling you to teach your children, and create a plan for moving forward in proactively teaching your children.

Courageous Parenting PODCAST

- Equipping Your Family for Spiritual Warfare (Ep. 349)

PRAYER

Father, we thank you for giving us Your Holy Spirit to guide us and provide us with insight. We pray for every parent reading this book to have the gift of spiritual discernment, that they might be able to distinguish between the spirits. We pray that they would have the courage to teach their children about spiritual warfare. Help us to be aware and alert, to be "as wise as serpents, but as harmless as doves" (Matt. 10:16). Thank you for giving us the full armor of God so that we might stand firm in your truth. We pray that You would raise a generation of people who yearn and thirst after You, who pursue holiness, and who have the insight to see an attack and to push forward without getting discouraged. God, we pray for a special anointing upon our children and their generation. May Your Kingdom come, and Your will be done on earth as it is in heaven. Amen.

CHAPTER 29

Apologetics and Evangelism

The biggest fear of many Christian parents lies in the unknown of the salvation of their children.

As we are talking about equipping our children for an uncertain world, one of the most important skills we can equip them with is the ability to communicate and defend their faith. The unsaved people of this world may not respect the religious, so we need to prepare our children to be able to communicate with skeptics, to express both a logical explanation of what they believe as well as a personal relationship with the God of the Universe.

Many parents unknowingly cultivate a religious culture in their home by their expectations, and by what they model, as well as what they do not live out. If children perceive that their parents' most profound concern is that they are the "perfect Christian," then they may become resentful of the church, the Bible, and possibly even God. As parents, we must be vigilant to remind our children that we care more about their hearts than their actions, while remembering that their actions reveal what is in their hearts! We also must reiterate this truth concerning what God cares most about as well!

For as the body apart from the spirit is dead, so also faith apart from works is dead." James 2:26

The truth is that our children will not have the desire to defend a faith they don't believe in themselves. They won't be motivated to share the gospel and evangelize to the lost if they have not experienced God and the saving grace of Jesus Christ. So, the first step in preparing our children is introducing them to God and showing them, by how we live, what seeking after God, and continuing to grow in Him can look like. When they acknowledge how powerful God's Spirit is in you, their parents, they are more likely to desire to experience Him too. Once our children desire to know God more, then we will witness them take personal responsibility for learning about Him.

So, yes, we must teach our children why we believe what we believe and teach them how to communicate that with others, but that must be secondary to facilitating and helping them to nurture a relationship with God as they grow up.

"But in your hearts honor Christ the Lord as holy, always being prepared to make a defense to anyone who asks you for a reason for the hope that is in you; yet do it with gentleness and respect," 1 Peter 3:15

Many parents do not feel qualified to teach apologetics, but that is a lie from the enemy. If God has called you, he will equip you. If you know how to read, then study the Word of God with your child. Just start right there. Ask your child or teen what questions they have about God and begin your search of who God is and what His Word says. As you model a love for God, His Word, and develop study skills, your children will be empowered to grow in the Lord as well. This is a time when humility is an asset.

If you do not know how to study the Bible, there are many good books that can teach you many different methods. Still, you can start by reading a few verses in Proverbs, stopping and thinking on it, looking up any words you don't know off the top of your head, and writing in a journal what those verses mean to you or how they apply to your life. Another way you can study Scripture is to read the word with the intent of just knowing God better. Begin looking for the attributes of God and pray through your reading, acknowledging His character and asking His Spirit to help you grow into the man or woman of God He designed you to be.

We're not saying classes or tutors are wrong; there are seasons and topics where this may be necessary and helpful. But instead of just sending your child to learn from someone else, may I challenge you to try to learn together? Disciple them. Be interested and thankful that they are interested too.

If you feel ill-equipped in defending your faith or discipling someone, then you need to dig in. Possibly find someone to disciple you as well. None of us has arrived, and we all need a Titus 2 Mentor in our lives. You cannot teach what you do not know, but God says that if we seek Him, we will find Him in Jeremiah 29:13.

To disciple our children well, we need to be personally investing in our spiritual growth and relationship with God. Our children will catch this, and then we have a platform on which to share the insights we have learned and they have learned to pass along a legacy of faith to our grandchildren, Lord willing.

Knowing how to defend one's faith is a big topic. I know it can be intimidating, but this is one of the most essential aspects we parents need to focus on in equipping our children for an uncertain world. This isn't as intense as it sounds. Those who don't know God need to know Him. We, and hopefully our children, get the honor of introducing Him to them! It's a matter of knowing God, knowing His Word, and sharing that with others.

The BEST way to equip your children for sharing about God with others is by modeling it for them.

Make reading the Bible a priority every day. Let them witness you sharing your faith and testimony of salvation with others. Jesus gave us an apparent model and example of how to disciple someone; you walk through life with them and teach them. And as you disciple your children, they will be learning how to disciple others. May I remind you, it's one of the main reasons we are here on earth.

Matthew 28:16-20 instructs us to go and make disciples of all nations. We are all called to partner with God in the fulfillment of the Great Commission. It's one of our corporate purposes as Christians, so we are charged and called by God to do it and train our children to as well.

In fact, the most important people to make disciples live in your home. Why would we spend time elsewhere if that's not happening by way of our own influence?

There's no church role, mission trip, or work evangelism that should come before the discipleship of our own children.

Parenting QUESTIONS

- ❖ Do you read your Bible daily? What do your children see?
- ❖ Do you share your faith with others?
- ❖ Would you be prepared to defend your faith if you needed to?
- ❖ What would you do if someone threatened or persecuted you because of your faith?
- ❖ Are you preparing your children to be able to answer these questions with confidence?

Courageous Parenting CHALLENGE

If you aren't already, examine your life and ask the questions:

- ❖ How could I be more Great Commission-focused?
- ❖ What does the Great Commission look like in my life?
- ❖ Have my children heard my salvation testimony? Have they witnessed me sharing it with others?
- ❖ Do they know how to share their faith? Have they been encouraged to pray for those they know who don't know Jesus? Start here! Pray together for those who are lost, for God to use you, give you an opportunity to share His story and the Truth!

Courageous Parenting PODCAST

- Handling Conflict & Disagreements that Uncertain Times Bring (Ep. 107)

PRAYER

God, we know that one of the main reasons You have created us is to know You and make You known. We realize it is our jurisdiction to prepare our children to be able to defend their faith as well as be a part of the TEAM called the Body of Christ. You call us all to make disciples. Would You give us the courage to obey You in this charge? Give us wisdom in how to train and equip our children for the Great Commission work. Direct the course, Lord. And help us to be supportive of our children in the ways they want to serve You, even if it seems dangerous. Please help us shoot the arrows You gave us. May they go far, strike hard, and fly straight toward the target. Cover us all in Your Armor, God, that it might extinguish all the flaming arrows of the evil one. Keep our feet fitted, ready in the gospel of peace, so that we can have the answers needed to win souls for your Kingdom!

For the Glory of Your Kingdom, Amen.

CHAPTER 30

Instill Stronger Resiliency to Trials

People often ask us how to prepare the next generation during a time of accelerating change and so many unknowns about what's ahead. If there were two things that are most important to encourage in your children, they would be an unwavering faith in Jesus and resiliency.

This next generation will be working and raising children in a changing landscape that's difficult to fully grasp, because we don't know what the world will be like in twenty years due to the accelerating technological advancements. But strong faith and a resilient spirit are crucial. So it's important to think about how your parenting encourages resiliency or curtails it.

They must be able to discern the wayward philosophies of the day to understand what's true, to be diligent problem solvers with a strong ability to overcome challenges, and be good at a lot of things, rather than becoming specialists in a few things. You can make a large difference in cultivating resiliency, and we believe it's more important than ever to do so.

Struggles, pains, and trials are going to occur in your child's lifetime. Everyone who walks this earth will journey through a valley, or two, before their life on earth is over. We must prepare our children for the realities of this life. Are you preparing your children to walk through the valley with unwavering faith in the Lord? Do your children see that in your life? Do they see you praising Him, even amid the trial? Often, it's the hardships of this life that reveal what we believe about ourselves and God.

God's Word asks us to count it all joy when we meet trials of various kinds (James 1:1-9) and exhorts us that by walking through trials Biblically, we will experience spiritual growth (Romans 5:3-5). God cares deeply about our character and wants us to be looking for opportunities to learn, grow, and glorify Him in all circumstances. This is an incredibly powerful truth that we must teach our children.

How does one prepare a son or daughter to walk through the toughest aspects of life in confidence with courage, looking for the lesson, and seeking God's face?

The answer is counter-cultural and challenging, but it will reap a bounty of strength in your children.

Don't shelter your children from every hardship you endure.

Use financial struggles, medical dilemmas, relationship issues, and other trials as teaching opportunities to anchor their faith and the conviction that life issues don't change the character of God. *Let your children witness you praise Him faithfully despite the trial.* We must model what it looks like to worship God while we are weeping and give Him thanks in the midst of grieving.

Many people today believe that children should be sheltered from financial problems, pain, loss, and sadness. The culture preaches the message, "Let children be children. Don't rob them of their innocent childhood."

A courageous parent instead says, "Don't rob your children of experiencing God as He guides you through trials."

Additionally, don't you want your children's prayers too?

The truth is that if you think your children are oblivious to the hardship you are walking through, you are naive. Children are remarkably observant and perceptive. How you handle yourself during struggles will teach your children a lot about life and mold their perspective on how they should react to life struggles in the future.

When we walked through our Job season, we lost almost everything we owned. We just had our seventh child, and we had to close the company we started that grew to forty three employees. We lost everything financially, with tremendous debt following us as well. We were counseled many times to claim bankruptcy, but we believed that we were reaping what we had sown and that we needed to do everything in our power to avoid that. During that season, the renter in our rental stopped paying, squatted on the property, stole our equipment and appliances, including our Kubota tractor, leading us to almost lose the property in foreclosure. That same weekend, while Angie was pregnant with our 8th, Selah, we went to clean and put our house and property on the market. Our baby died, but we didn't find out until a month later, when Angie suffered but survived a serious miscarriage where she lost over sixty-seven percent of her blood and almost died.

We're sharing the cliff note version with you here, but through it all, we were faced with the choice to be transparent with our children and chose to give praise to God and focus on Him, His blessings, and to pray or to keep it to ourselves out of an intention of protecting our children. We chose to be transparent and humble with our children, and they grew tremendously because of it. Our family had never been closer. It was hard, but the spiritual maturity that we now see from that season is priceless. And though we would never wish what we walked through to happen to anyone, we wouldn't ask God to change a thing about what we walked through. We saw prayers answered and experienced what it feels like to be carried by the Body of Christ. Our children experienced the Biblical Church the way it was meant to be. Our whole family grew closer to God and one another through the trials, suffering, and pain of loss. A lot died in that season, including our pride, and we praise God for that.

Teach them how to Grieve Biblically

Do you believe this scripture? "I can do all things through him who strengthens me." Philippians 4:13

Do your children see you doing all things through Christ, who gives you strength? Or do they see you constantly striving in your own strength?

We mentioned in the last chapter that your children would undoubtedly experience hardship and trials in their lifetime. In fact, they are likely to face even more challenging things in their future. They need to be more resilient and more trusting of the Lord in their circumstances than the past generations of modern times.

Another pain we all experience is loss.

Your children will encounter heartache and loss, and unfortunately, today's American culture doesn't allow people to grieve. It isn't patient, compassionate, or empathetic with those grieving. This is one reason why people are so desensitized to the truth regarding human rights, life, and death. When we distance ourselves from the pain that comes with loss, we stuff it deep down inside.

God calls us to embrace and engage the loss, not stuff it or move on without emotion.

When we suffered pregnancy loss, our oldest three children were all teenagers, which added a whole new element to the grieving process. Not only were we grieving the loss of a baby, but so were they. We clung to Scripture and sought to more deeply know God's character during that time.

As a woman in grief, I remember feeling so weak physically and having to rely on the Lord to sustain me. I deeply desired to find the purpose in my suffering and the trial of loss, and I was also deeply aware that I was modeling for my children how to walk through the valley of the shadow of death Biblically. I desired to grow in Him and understand His Word more. I sought healing in the deepest wounds of my heart and mind, knowing only God could heal my broken Mama's heart. But I also wanted to leave a legacy of how to engage hard life trials in a way that glorified God above the pain.

1 Thessalonians 4:13-18 spoke volumes to me as a Christian grieving loss. Of course, it reinforced that we grieve, unlike the world, because we have a hope that our beloved is with God in Heaven.

> *"For godly grief produces a repentance that leads to salvation without regret, whereas worldly grief produces death."*
>
> 2 Corinthians 7:10

If we are in the world but called not to be of it, then our grief will look different than the culture we live in. This was one eye-opening example of how our view of children being a blessing from God impacted how we grieved differently from the world. In a world that does not value a baby's life, we will grieve the loss because we do. Every child is a gift, an eternal inheritance, a reward, a treasure in heaven.

> *"Blessed are those who mourn, for they shall be comforted."*
>
> Matthew 5:4

We cried, we wept, and we allowed and invited others to weep with us, but we also took action to bring glory to God by how we responded. It was our love offering. In this time of tremendous physical suffering and loss, we chose to teach our children how to grieve biblically, which required us to learn more. We learned that grief after losing someone isn't something that should be avoided. No matter how people try to push it away or ignore it, the pain will affect them. How it affects them is determined by what they believe and the depth of their faith. Tears were not made to be hidden. Hiding has always been an act of self-preservation provoked by sin. Honest tears are a confession of pain, and pain is not a sin. Sometimes the pain you experience is a consequence of sin, but the pain is not a sin. When you try to suppress your emotions and hide them from others, what is it you're trying to preserve? Are you protecting your ego? When you die, do you want those you loved to hide their tears? Do you want them to try to forget about you? Do you want your family to hide from the pain of losing you? If the answer to these questions is no, then we must be willing to stop, grieve, weep, and allow others to weep with us.

Grieve together. Show your children that there is no shame in mourning. But remember to surrender your pain and grief to God. Remember to praise Him. Remember your hope.

God's Word encourages us to have a legacy mindset.

> *"Blessed be the God and Father of our Lord Jesus Christ, the Father of mercies and God of all comfort, who comforts us in all our affliction, so that we may be able to comfort those who are in any affliction, with the comfort with which we ourselves are comforted by God."*
>
> 2 Corinthians 1:3-4

If there was ever a redemptive purpose for walking through the valley of the shadow of death, that is it. That God might be glorified as He enables us to react counter-culturally, shining a light on Him. God doesn't promise us that this life won't have pain, but He does promise us that He will walk with us through it.

> **Disclaimer:** We're not recommending sharing all gory details of relationship trauma, divorce, and all financial trials. As a parent, you do need to ask for wisdom from the Lord and use discretion. We need to make the most out of EVERY opportunity to prepare and teach our children.

Imagine how the faith of a child can grow if they are aware of financial hardship and watch God answer their prayers and work miracles. Imagine how powerful and memorable it could be for a child to be praying for a friend or family member to know Jesus, and then they get to witness Christ transform them!

Parenting QUESTIONS

- Have you walked through a hard season in your life?
- How did you cope with it when no one else was looking except your family?
- Do you tend to hide the truth from your children and live a facade, or do you share prayer requests and honestly lead them to the throne room in prayer?
- Are you humble before your children? Do you share with them when you make mistakes that end in unfortunate circumstances? We must let our children learn from our mistakes and make sure that we don't just brush the truth under the rug.
- Do your children see you walking by faith in all seasons and journeys in life?

Remember, God cares about the little things, too.

Vulnerability and humility will win a loyal and faithful son/daughter over. Remember that what you walk through today in your life might be redeemed later in life because your child has developed a spiritual and mental toughness from witnessing how you handled life trials.

Courageous Parenting CHALLENGE

- Is there something you are hiding from your spouse or children because you are ashamed?
- Is God asking you to share that burden or hurt with them so they can carry the load with you, learn from you, and grow closer to one another and God?

- ❖ The truth is that those who labor together build stronger bonds. Don't believe the lie that you need to do this all on your own.

Courageous Parenting PODCAST

- Grieving Loss When Your Kids Are Watching (Ep. 293)
- Wisdom on Suffering Through Miscarriage (Ep. 63)
- How to Parent Through Life Trials & Financial Struggles (Ep. 5)

PRAYER

Lord, we want to be more like You and are convicted to always grow in humility. Give us the courage to share the lessons we learn with our children as Your Spirit directs us. Help us be vulnerable so that they might be more prepared for the valleys they will undoubtedly experience in life. Give us wisdom in how to lead our children through the hardships and suffering they may face. Help us to be full of mercy and compassion when they need it, and fill our minds with understanding when we need to guide them. Thank you for being our comfort, our deliverer in times of trial, and our shepherd as we walk through the valleys of this life, Lord. We love you and are so grateful. Amen.

CHAPTER 31

More Courage is Required

Congratulations on getting here. You are truly an intentional parent who understands that we are living in unprecedented times. In this final chapter, we will give you encouragement, ideas for implementation, and things you can do to get your marriage even more aligned in being Courageous Parents who influence the right changes to help your children thrive in a vastly different future.

This book isn't meant to be a quick read that you move on from, but instead an ongoing encouragement to take the path less traveled by. Whether you come back to find the podcast link on a certain subject, use a chapter for a date night discussion, or need a refresher as you navigate new issues, consider this a useful handbook.

There's a lot in this book, and we do believe it's all really important for equipping children to thrive in unprecedented times. However, it may feel like a daunting task to implement these thirty-one principles all at once.

We are sure you'd agree that the goal isn't just knowledge of what to do, but instead ongoing implementation of these principles to influence a thriving legacy.

But here's a big WARNING: Don't try to change everything at once. At least one of you in the marriage will get overwhelmed by that, leading to inaction. That would be playing the short game; desiring changes so badly that you try to change everything at once. It's short-sighted because it will make it difficult for you to implement in alignment as a married couple as well.

The result will likely be discouragement and inaction. In other words, it likely leads to short-lived implementation, which doesn't change anything.

Instead, you want to be like dripping water.

Think of you and your spouse as two water sources that join together and drip in the exact same spot.

Dripping water that never stops over a long period of time will cause dramatic change to the surface below, regardless of how hardened the material is. Or in your case, no matter how independent or stubborn your children are.

We've said for years that parenting is a long-game, just like dripping water has little effect for a short period of time, so do your parenting efforts. Also, like water, you won't see the changes right away, but over time, huge changes happen.

In fact, dripping water over a long period of time can completely transform the earth and stone below it.

The same is true of parents who are intentional in the right directions consistently and in marriage in unison, over a long period of time. This must include a commitment together in asking the Lord to give you wisdom, courage, and to reach your children's hearts.

Here's another WARNING, though; if your marriage is dripping in different directions, it can cause the landscape to have a very different outcome, which could also be true for your legacy.

There are probably five kinds of people reading this book, and here's encouragement for all of you.

The first is someone who's married, and both parents are intentional, hungry to grow, willing to change, and on an active journey together to become stronger biblical parents. Unfortunately, THIS IS VERY RARE.

You are both on a healthy path, and it will be the easiest for you to implement the areas in this book that can strengthen your parenting and marriage teamwork even more. A potential challenge for some could be pride. If that's you, it could lead to its own set of issues and cause blind spots in your parenting and marriage over time.

In reading this book, you likely have become aware of opportunities for growth. We encourage you to have your spouse read it as well as to discuss these opportunities to encourage your marriage to leave an even stronger legacy.

Second is someone who's an intentional parent, but their spouse is less active and more passive when it comes to parenting. Unfortunately THIS IS VERY COMMON.

This is what exists in most Christian marriages, and even though it's common, the passive parent must be encouraged to wake up. If this is your situation, pray for your spouse consistently on this and get alone time together to discuss. A passive parent likely didn't see courageous parenting modeled, may have difficulty in understanding how to insert themselves, or they are assuming everything is good because of delegating to coaches, youth pastors, and other teachers.

Additionally, it could be a sign of hidden marriage challenges as well. Are you both embracing biblical gender roles well? Is there clear communication about jurisdictions and how to work as a team? Have you discussed how to pass the parenting baton well to each other? Do you have a biblically sound parenting plan you are both committed to implementing together?

Here is the resource that has helped thousands of intentional parents get there together: The Parenting Mentor Program. Learn more at courageousparenting.com.

Third is someone who's an intentional parent, but their spouse sees things completely differently, and perhaps isn't a Christian at all. There IS HOPE.

While this is a difficult situation, and of course, it's going to be easier when both spouses are in alignment, it doesn't mean a legacy of fruitfulness is lost. Quite the opposite, in fact, the future fruit of your diligent and loving efforts to disciple your children in the way they should go could be the very thing someday that causes your spouse to embrace Jesus as their Lord and Savior.

Your path is harder, but so was Eunice's path. Eunice was Timothy's mother in the Bible, and Timothy was an invaluable leader in the first-century church, commissioned by Paul himself to correct false teaching and establish leadership in the Church in Ephesus. Did you know her husband wasn't a believer? The bible credits Eunice and his grandmother Lois for discipling Timothy.

Fourth is someone who's an intentional parent, but there is no spouse. You are doing this alone, but don't be discouraged, there IS HOPE.

Another very hard path, but a worthy one. You probably feel the weight of doing everything yourself, but the Lord will sustain you if you keep trusting and following Him. When it comes to Spiritual discipleship, your voice needs to stay powerful in the minds of your children, so it's vital to do all you can, which includes garnering the support of trusted older people with wisdom in your church as well.

You don't have to be alone in this; pray daily for the right influences to come into your lives that are trustworthy and helpful. Find a church where people are willing to connect with you and help.

An interesting thing to think about is the value of keeping your children with you during church service. We believe that's important regardless, but it also lets people see you as a diligent single parent being super intentional. There will be more opportunities for other older people to connect with your children, too.

Fifth is someone who hasn't been an intentional parent and may have any of the other four scenarios with their spouse. Be encouraged, IT'S NOT TOO LATE.

We won't sugarcoat things; your passivity will echo into the future negatively in your legacy if you stay on that course. There's a battle for your child's heart, and the enemy has more tools than ever to capture it. No matter what has happened in your family so far, it's not too late. You can start standing in the gap, and over time, it will make a huge difference in your children's lives.

You may be wondering what your first steps should be.

- Repent to God for your passivity in this area, as it's a direct disobedience to the Lord's instruction for parents.
- Ask God for wisdom and help in becoming an intentional parent.
- Go on a date with your spouse and share the convictions in your heart, and apologize to your spouse for causing them to carry the weight. Ask for your spouse's prayer and encouragement as you take steps to be more proactive. Ask your spouse for feedback on areas that would be best to start being more proactive.
- Meet with your children in humility, apologize for whatever is needed, and give a vision for how things will be changing. This can also help set new expectations for them as well.
- Do one new thing that rejects passivity and embraces your God-given role, and don't stop. That one thing will become a catalyst for more things as you get traction.

There is nothing else that matters as much as you making these changes.

Courageous parenting isn't for the faint of heart, as it will cause you to be unpopular at times. It will cause confusion in others' minds, as some close to you won't understand your choices. It could risk relationships with others who take a personal offense to your more biblical choices.

You can't deny that normal Christian parenting rhythms are largely failing in society. If you want different outcomes, you have to make different choices. If your parenting looks like most people in your church, you likely aren't on the right path.

Don't let yourself be pacified by your environment, meaning, don't let your standards be lowered, don't go along to get along when the spirit is prompting you to do something different. Don't operate in fear of others; instead, lead your environment by your counterintuitive actions. Be an example, and some will follow, and others won't; they might even mock you behind your back.

Were they real friends if that's true?

The goal is to preserve and nurture strong relationships with everyone, but never at the sacrifice of the long-term well-being and spiritual health of your children. If there's an issue, go to the person in love and discuss it.

If you truly do it lovingly with humility, not haughtiness, you will find it strengthens your relationship. But if it causes harm to the relationship, be encouraged, as you are discovering that perhaps your relationship was shallow and on shaky ground to begin with.

So many people come and go in life, but your family is your family. The children you are parenting right now are the ones that will either further a faith-filled legacy through their own families and beyond or not. You have the most influence over it. Unfortunately, too many parents are thinking short-term and don't realize that they are sacrificing their future legacy's health for today's friendships.

If they are real friends, they will listen and try to understand, and it will likely sharpen them too. It also grows relationships where they can also do that with you down the road if needed. You want friends like that!

Additionally, if you tolerate lower standards around your children, you'll have a hard time attracting the kind of friendships you can truly run the race with those who would embrace the concepts in this book. To them, you will look like the group you are running with, causing confusion in their minds.

Now, don't get us wrong, we absolutely are to be loving to all people, to share

Too many parents are thinking short-term and don't realize that they are sacrificing their future legacy's health for today's friendships.

the gospel and be a witness for Christ, but you can do that without sacrificing your children.

So yes, you will have people in different places in their lives spiritually, but you will do things in ways where your children don't get harmed. Too many children are harmed in the name of ministry.

Our families are our first and foremost ministry; everything else comes after that.

Here are some tips for implementing this book:

PRAY

Realize that we are all on a journey with different situations and family dynamics. It's not about what has happened; it's about what's ahead because you are making changes. Be encouraged and remember that the Lord is worthy of our trust, loves you and your family, knows the desires of your heart, and wants to do wonderful things through your family. Your job is to stay in His will, trust and obey Him.

Ask the Lord in prayer for His will to be done and for wisdom on what your next steps should be!

NO FEAR

Don't make parenting decisions in fear. If you stay surrendered to the Lord and his will, you won't, but if you start operating more in your own flesh, then fear will grow. It's a lack of trust in God, and most decisions made in fear end up backfiring in some way later. In fact, two people can make the same decision, but if one is in fear and the other is in wisdom, they will likely experience different outcomes. Why is that? The one who made the decision in wisdom is listening to the Lord, and the other one is listening to their fear. Those are very different things that usually carve different paths over time.

SHORT LIST

Make a short list of what you want to implement. You may need to scan back through the book and create an action list, then prioritize a few things that you believe are most important to start with. If it applies to you, then meet with your spouse and discuss. (Ideally, have your spouse read the book as well and have them make a list, and then compare as you meet.

Remember, if it's possible, you want to be dripping in the same direction to influence change. It's highly possible that if there are good intentions, but poor communication, you both don't even realize your water isn't dripping in the same spot.

The Courageous Parenting Charge!

Whether you are the father or mother, the most important mission God has for you is in your home. All fruitfulness should be an overflow of what's happening in your home. The world will tempt you to gradually shift your priorities, so it's vital to constantly recalibrate and keep your family the main thing.

It's so much easier to be excited about the times we are living in if you know you are equipping your children to thrive in the different future ahead. Those who stay in the normal Christian rhythms are either naive or fearful. Don't let that be you, NO, YOU ARE A COURAGEOUS PARENT!

COURAGEOUS PARENTS believe that these are the greatest times to be alive, because these are the times God wanted you to be here, these are the times God wanted your children to be here, and God made you your children's parents on purpose.

We get to live and parent through the largest societal changes in the history of the world. When you embrace it, you approach it correctly. When you fear it, you won't. It's that simple.

Leave the fear behind and simply take one new step forward at a time while trusting the Lord. Never stop growing, implementing, and praying. Watch the Lord do a work in your family beyond your expectations.

You are raising the next generation of Godly people to be lights for Christ during extraordinary times.

Trust in the Lord while being courageous, brothers and sisters, and watch that Godly courage extend through your legacy, regardless of the times ahead.

Courageous Parenting Podcast:

- Don't Grow Weary in Doing Good (Ep. 43)
- Courage Lived Leads to Courageous Kids Launched (Ep. 298)

SECTION FOUR

Marriage Challenge

Begin your date night in prayer together, reflecting on the last section of the book, you likely have been able to pinpoint or narrow down some topics of discussion for tonight. Maybe you have a child that is struggling with being disrespectful, or a child that has zero motivation in school, maybe a child struggling with night terrors or scary dreams, or maybe you feel ill equipped to train your children in biblical worldview apologetics, or maybe you are walking through a trying time as a family and needed that encouragement on walking through life trials biblically and growing in resiliency?

PRAYER

Heavenly Father, You have created our family for a purpose, and we want to live for You. We are beyond grateful for the sacrifice You made so that we can be made new, forgiven, and live with You forever in eternity. Our greatest desire is that our children would grow up to know and love You deeply. Give us wisdom and discernment in our parenting decisions, Lord. We pray that Your will would be done in our children's lives and that You would protect our family from evil and forgive us when we fall short. Help us to forgive others in our parenting journey and protect our family relationships so that we can be the team You designed us to be. We pray that you would keep our eyes open to see what You see and pray for the people and situations that break Your heart. Lead our children in life everlasting, and keep them from temptation. May Your will be done and May You Be Glorified. In Jesus' Name, Amen.

Here are the sections of Chapter Three to discuss

Spiritual Maturity & Battle Ready

1. Discipled for Wise Decision Making
2. Trained in Weapons of Righteousness
3. Help Their Respectfulness Rise
4. Cultivate a Hunger for Learning
5. Equipped for Spiritual Warfare
6. Apologetics and Evangelism
7. Instill Stronger Resiliency to Trials
8. More Courage is Required

Discussion Questions:

- What are the areas that are the most important for you to grow in stronger alignment in your parenting?
- What is your most pressing parenting concern right now?
- If you were to give yourself a grade on equipping your children for unprecedented times, what would it be?

Marriage Challenge:

Knowledge is nice, but implementation is almost everything. Your influence on your family only improves by the level of implementation that actually happens consistently over a long period of time.

We encourage you to go on a date night and discuss the three questions above, review your short list of most important things to implement, and align together in implementing them.

We highly encourage you to pray together and for your initiatives as well.

Parenting can be discouraging, especially when you realize there's a lot to do. Be encouraged in that no matter what's happening or where things are at, it's never too late, and you can lead your family to stronger places.

Real change isn't about gushing water for a short period of time; the real difference is in drips concentrated in one direction over a long period of time. Too many people respond to new information with overwhelm that leads to inaction, changing nothing, or too much implementation all at once, which is too much for everyone to handle, leaving them with short-lived dreams.

Be Courageous!

One of the most powerful marriage alignment resources that thousands of parents have utilized is the Parenting Mentor Program. This is an ideal next step together (Single parents are welcome too), and you can learn more at courageousparenting.com.

You can find all ministry resources at becourageousministry.org as well.

ABOUT THE AUTHORS

In 26 years of marriage Isaac and Angie have experienced every season of parenting with nine children, from babies to married adult children, and now they have a rising number of grandchildren while their youngest is four. As sought after speakers on marriage and family they also host the Christian podcast, Courageous Parenting. Isaac is the Church planting pastor of Rooted Bible Church and hosts the Resolute Man podcast. Angie is a veteran homeschool mom, bible teacher, and the author of *Redeeming Childbirth.* and many online Bible studies. As founders of becourageousministry.org, they've coached thousands of parents through their parenting mentor program on mission to impact 10 million legacies for God's glory.

ENDNOTES

i https://www.barna.com/research/resilient-disciples/
ii http://slightlineministry.org
iii https://williamsinstitute.law.ucla.edu/press/transgender-estimate-press-release/
iv https://www.barna.com/research/resilient-disciples/

www.ingramcontent.com/pod-product-compliance
Lightning Source LLC
LaVergne TN
LVHW010650110826
845149LV00014B/3018

* 9 7 9 8 9 9 5 9 2 0 8 0 9 *